A Sunset Discovery Book

GOLD RUSH
COUNTRY

A Sunset Discovery Book

GOLD RUSH COUNTRY

Guide to California's Mother Lode and Northern Mines

BY THE EDITORS OF SUNSET BOOKS AND SUNSET MAGAZINE

Foreword by Oscar Lewis

LANE BOOKS, MENLO PARK, CALIFORNIA

Acknowledgments

No book of this sort could have been written without the help of interested and qualified people—those who supplied raw material and later checked the rough manuscript. We are indeed indebted to many who have contributed their assistance.

We are particularly grateful for the help given by the following: the staff at Columbia Historic State Park—Curators H. E. Rensch and Hubert R. McNoble, Supervisor Lester M. Ransom—and other staff members of the State Division of Parks and Beaches at Sacramento; Judge J. A. Smith of San Andreas; Leta M. Rosebrook of Oroville; May Perry, curator of the Placer County Museum in Auburn; William Wintle of Volcano; Axel Gravender of Grass Valley; Donald I. Segerstrom and Mrs. H. Paul Burden of Sonora; Ross F. Taylor of Downieville; and C. F. Huntington of Oroville for information on the suspension bridge at Bidwells Bar.

A special note of thanks must go to the good people of the county and city chambers of commerce through the Gold Country for their very necessary aid not only in supplying information and checking, but in referring us to other experts to assist us in this project.

Library of Congress Catalog Card Number 63-7787

Second Edition

Fifth Printing January 1967

Title No. 625

Copyright © 1957, 1963

LANE MAGAZINE & BOOK COMPANY, MENLO PARK, CALIFORNIA

By the publishers of *Sunset* Books and *Sunset*, the Magazine of Western Living

Lithographed in the U.S.A.

Foreword

The event that first focused on California the rapt attention of the rest of the world was, of course, Jim Marshall's finding of a few flakes of yellow metal in the tailrace of Captain Sutter's new sawmill beside the American River. What happened during the next half-dozen years forms one of the most dramatic chapters in the nation's history. For a horde of Argonauts, traveling by land and water, converged on California from all points of the compass, and in their ardent hunt for gold explored every nook and cranny of the Sierra foothills from Mariposa northward to Mount Shasta and beyond.

During their brief stay in the Mother Lode country, the gold hunters left an impress on the land that a full century has failed to erase. To be sure, during the hundred years that have elapsed since then, many changes have occurred. Some of the once populous early-day camps have disappeared entirely; the sites of others are marked only by heaps of rubble and a few ruined walls, while yet others have become prosperous towns, their streets lined with substantial modern buildings of brick or stone.

With this fine book on the arm of his comfortable chair or the seat of his moving car, the reader can better "travel through" the exciting past of the Gold Rush Country. It is in one volume a solid contribution to both Western travel literature and Californiana. For those who today venture into the area, whether by armchair or automobile, will find on its pages precisely that information, briefly and authentically set forth, that will enable them to understand and appreciate the abundance of historical lore that still clings to virtually every stream, every town, and every abandoned campsite. Without some such mentor, much of the romance of the region would surely be missed; with it, it becomes easy to seek out those relics of the past that enable one to visualize the stirring events which took place there a century or more ago.

Incidentally, it is altogether appropriate that this excellent guidebook to the Mother Lode country should have been compiled and issued by the publishers of *Sunset* Magazine. For *Sunset,* ever since its founding well over a half century ago, has devoted itself to chronicling the attractions of life in the West, and although it has been mainly concerned with the contemporary scene, from time to time it has turned backward to reveal to present-day readers some phase of the region's eventful past.

OSCAR LEWIS

Table of Contents

───

◄ **At left,** the Lavezzo Building in Volcano has stout iron doors to protect it from fire. It was once a wine shop, but the last entry in its ledger was made before the turn of the century. **The cover** shows Firehouse No. I in Nevada City. Over a century old, the building is now a museum. **On the title page** is the Fallon House in Columbia. A one-time hotel, it is now used as a summer theater by the University of the Pacific, Stockton.

Introduction —

to California's Golden Past

Five months before California became one of the United States of America, the Free State of Rough and Ready, fed up with damyankees, taxes, and the bothersome long haul to the county seat, seceded from both California and the United States. A decade later, Rough and Ready's gold was pouring into Washington to help preserve the Union. In view of a more significant secession, the Free State's declaration of independence was forgotten, even in the rambunctious little principality itself.

In 1848, after it applied for a United States post office for the second time, Rough and Ready finally received its ultimatum: join up or do without. The Confederate States of America lasted less than 5 years, the Republic of Texas barely 10; the Free State of Rough and Ready came back into the fold just 2 years short of its centennial.

It's odd bits of history like this that keep the Gold Rush alive for most of us. We remember that it wasn't *Tom Sawyer* or *Innocents Abroad* that made Mark Twain famous in his own day; it was a jumping frog from Calaveras County. We read Bret Harte and his successors, and think of the gold era in terms of anecdotes and characters.

The kind of story telling that needed the fantastic, the bizarre, the superlative, and, for accent, the occasional diminutive, found fertile soil in the Gold Country. Extremes were the order of the day, and the point is not so much whether a story is true or not; the fact remains that the wildest tales could have been true, and for every one that can't be proved, there are a dozen untold ones that could be.

RAW GOLD IN HUGE CHUNKS

You can believe almost anything about a country where gold turned up in chunks weighing as much as 195 pounds; where a letter would go 200 miles in a day by Pony Express; where you paid a dollar for a slice of bread and another dollar to butter it; where cities grew overnight and disappeared almost as quickly; where in a few short months, thousands of square miles were laced with flumes, rivers and mountains were reshaped, moved around, or done away with, and promising communities in the coastal valleys became ghost towns as their inhabitants rushed off to the placer mines.

You need to know some of the superlatives, at least, before you go looking at the Gold Country today, because you'll find thin evidence there of what it really was. True, the 1850's did leave relics scattered across the miles between the Feather River and the San Joaquin. The wonder of it all, though, is not that the Forty-Niners and those who followed left as much as they did, but that there is really so little to show for their earth-shaking migration or their incredible industry.

You do see a century-old building here and there, and once in a great while a sizable cluster of them, and you drive over miles of the havoc wrought by the hydraulic Monitors, but even the most dramatic diggings are now softened by pines and manzanita. There's hardly so much as a stick left, for example, of the 300 miles of flumes on San Juan Ridge, and it doesn't mean much to pause and look at the shiny headframe of the Empire Mine unless you know something about its 200 miles of underground workings, its main shaft boring 11,000 feet into the earth, and the wealth and organization that have kept it pouring out its golden millions through wars and government restrictions and sharply rising costs.

IT LASTED JUST TEN YEARS

The Gold Rush did get well under way in 1849, a year or so after Marshall's discovery at Coloma, and within ten years it had dwindled to a point where the abrupt eastward emigration to Nevada's Comstock Lode was hardly more than a *coupe de grace*. By then the stream beds had been sifted thoroughly, not once but over and over again, first by impatient miners anxious to try their luck and move on to greener—or golder—pastures, then by Chinese gleaners who picked over the placers once more, mile by mile, inch by inch, pebble by pebble. By the time young Mark Twain arrived in 1864, Eldorado was already a land of ruins.

Then it took capital and a good deal of imagination to get the gold. Ancient rivers had piled their gravels hundreds of feet deep; the way to get at the riches held fast in the gravel mountains was to break down the mountains, and the inexorable cutting blasts of water from the Monitors did just that, and would be doing it yet if they hadn't been stopped by law in 1884. The reason: the melted mountains were ending up in the agricultural valleys, destroying farms and homes and ruining navigation on the rivers that had run deep and clear before the Argonauts arrived. It's no figure of speech to say that communities in the hydraulic districts died overnight with the advent of the Anti-Debris Act; they did exactly that, and those that hadn't already been washed away by their own nozzles, or haven't been burned down or cannibalized for lumber since, are among the least altered of all the gold towns.

AFTER THE MONITORS WERE SILENCED

The third phase of the gold business was lode mining, the extraction of gold from mother ores—one of two methods that produce importantly today. It started early but didn't come into its own until the pick-and-shovel and hydraulic days were nearly over, and skilled engineering and vast capital backing were available. The headframes—triangular scaffolds of steel or timber—that you see against the sky throughout the Gold Country mark the shafts of the hardrock mines that quickly brought California's gold production figures from millions of dollars into the hundreds of millions. In 1941, 175 of them were still operating; today only a handful around Grass Valley and a scattered half dozen elsewhere are active.

Along some of the rivers still, the "bottom of the barrel" is being scraped by rattling dredges that scoop deep into the water-worn aggregates and turn over enough rock to show a profit from stream-bed debris worth as little as 20 cents per cubic yard. It's a far cry from days when a miner might find a single nugget worth $5,000 or $50,000 or $73,710 (California's record find). And when you understand how thoroughly every square foot of ground in thousands of square miles of Gold Country was searched, and how carefully every likely square foot was crushed and screened and washed and searched again,

you realize that this serene land, even with its fading movie-set facades, its quaint towns so self-consciously proud of themselves as molders of destiny, and its hundreds of commemorative tablets striving valiantly to keep the past alive, is a far cry from what it was in the busier, noisier, dustier, untidier days of '49.

The Gold Rush left the West's biggest endowment of history that still shows. Over most of the Gold Country, history shows just about enough, but still not so much that the fun of seeking it out is lost. You won't find many things actually dating back to 1849, because there simply weren't many *things* around (including buildings) at that time, and the few structures that were erected were so flimsy that they haven't survived. Cornerstones and gravestones tell you that the Gold Country, foreseeing no end to its fortunes, built and buried well by the middle Fifties.

JACKSON TAILING WHEELS NOW RELICS

Some of the relics aren't really old at all, but they are bona fide relics just the same. If it is disillusioning to learn that the famous Jackson tailing wheels are products of the 20th Century, remember that their life history is finished nevertheless; they've been strictly Californiana since their electric motors whined to a halt in 1934, and the chronicle of California gold—well into its anticlimax but still not finished—needs them for completeness as it needed the fandango halls, Lotta Crabtree, and Black Bart, and as it will need the modern stamp mills when the last one goes out of business.

The Gold Country we talk about—the area shown on the map following page 32—doesn't comprise all of the gold-bearing land in California. It doesn't include the rich diggings of the Weaverville area, or even the spot where gold was first discovered in what is now the Golden State. Near Los Angeles, probably as early as 1834, gold was found, and the mission padres had modest placer operations under way from 1842 to 1846. But the Mother Lode and the Northern Mines, the hazily separate areas we discuss and illustrate here as a unit, make up the major gold belt, appropriately traversed by State Highway 49.

Maybe you've dipped into the Gold Country on your way somewhere else. Maybe you've taken the length of Highway 49 in one big bite; if so, you may have had your fill of stone walls and iron shutters and little else, but you probably learned that it's easy to become well informed on the Gold Rush if you're psychic enough to know which authority to believe.

YOU'LL FIND MARKERS IN ABUNDANCE

Plaques and signs sometimes disagree with each other and almost invariably are disputed by the local old-timers who seem to appear every time you unfold a road map or focus a camera. The Division of Highways, the various county historical societies, and the Native Sons and Daughters of the Golden West, and others have erected scores of bronze markers at or near historic spots, and you can practically reconstruct the gold era for yourself by stopping and reading each one you see.

But the gold region will mean much more to you if you visit your library first and discover the wealth of absorbing literature that the land and its people have inspired. Some of the quietest rural landscapes come to rollicking life if someone in the car keeps tab on the miles and reads the fitting passages from Joseph Henry Jackson's *Anybody's Gold,* for example, as you travel. And winding down to nondescript Rich Bar after sampling the *Shirley Letters* is like going home.

Some of the old things require no literary build-up. It's enough, for instance, to stand in a present-day courtroom in Mariposa and know that, except for the electric lights, it has remained virtually unchanged since it saw its first trial, seven years before the inauguration of Abraham Lincoln.

RIVER BOTTOM TO MOUNTAIN TOP

The Gold Country ranges in altitude from rolling grassland a few hundred feet above sea level to the 6,700-foot elevation of fir-clad, often snowy Yuba Pass. Highway 49 stays at around 2,000 feet, except where it dips into the deep canyons of the rivers it crosses, and where it climbs up the Yuba above Downieville. In summer, weather at the lower altitudes is likely to be hot, but as you climb into the digger pine belt and beyond into higher levels, you'll find it mellow and calm. The dust probably will be deep on the unpaved logging roads, and on the leaves and grass beside them, as it was along the thoroughfares traveled by the Concord coaches of the Central Overland Stage. But when fall arrives, the first rains come to lay the dust and wash the oaks, poplars, locusts, and eastern maples in time for them to brighten the old towns with yellow and vermilion.

In winter, rain turns the red foothill soil to mud, and snow covers the higher altitudes. You'll be restricted to the main roads, generally, but most of the Gold Country towns are on maintained routes.

At the lower elevations, spring comes along as the days begin to lengthen noticeably in February and March —and you cut right across the Gold Country on a trip to the snow from the Bay Area or from Marysville, Sacramento, Stockton, or Modesto. In April and May, the snowbanks still lean against the leaning buildings of La Porte and Graniteville, and the back roads are as deep with mud as they were with dust in September, but the tide of wildflowers that sweeps over the green countryside is something to behold. If you'd like hills of fairy lanterns and mile on mile of blazing Scotch broom with your antiques, you'll want to return in the spring. Countless blooms of lupine, owl's clover, Mariposa lily, buttercup, brodiaea, and the glorious California poppy paint the hills as days grow longer.

BE SURE TO TAKE A CAMERA

The photographic possibilities in the Gold Country are endless and decidedly underworked. You might try for closeups, details, anonymous "atmosphere"—the things you don't find on the picture postcards. In some places you'll find the old practically smothered by the new—old buildings, still in use, decorated with neon signs or flanked by discouraging modern structures.

If you're the kind of purist who can't tolerate this sort of thing, you'll be disappointed—camera-wise, at least—in the largest towns. Even out in the country, you'll find many of the old buildings functioning comfortably under incongruous roofs of glaring aluminum or slightly mellower corrugated iron. Except in painstakingly restored Columbia and a few of the most tourist-conscious places, the tendency is for the Gold Rush mementoes to disappear—through modernization, razing, or decay (see pages 39 and 50, top). For quiet-looking streets and a minimum of parked cars obscuring the watering troughs and scrollwork, get out *early* on a Sunday morning with your camera.

Not all of Highway 49 is pretty. The outskirts of some of the larger towns, for example, were not planned for sightseers. But the brief passages of ugliness are forgotten when you hit the country-lane stretch between Cool and Pilot Hill, or the spectacular switchbacks between Bear Valley and Bagby. And the minor side roads, many of them as good to drive on as Highway 49 itself, lead to and through many a scene of unsullied charm. Lumber and cattle are economic mainstays of the Gold Country now; you'll see log ponds and sawmills, and occasionally you'll encounter a traffic-stalling herd ambling down the road in front of a cowboy or two.

MUCH INFORMATION IS AVAILABLE

In the principal towns, call on the chambers of commerce for information. They often have maps and printed guides for free distribution. City halls, hotels, motels, and restaurants are other places where informative brochures are frequently available. Probably nowhere is data dispensed so generously and enthusiastically as in this tradition-proud land, and no wonder: the golden legend can never die, and there will be travelers to seek it out when the last ponderosa has been felled and the last dogie has eaten the last wild oat.

Museums—good ones—are everywhere. Visit as many as you have time for. Along the highways you can buy useful antiques, second-hand junk, Gold Country relics and souvenirs, and even raw gold.

If you want to set a record, you can probably drive the 270 twisting miles of Golden Highway between Mariposa and Sattley in a day, but you won't see much and your tires and temper will surely suffer. A long weekend will let you pause at the markers and absorb a smattering of lore, with no time out for picture-taking. You can make a pretty thorough reconnaissance of Highway 49 in a week, but you would need twice as much time to include the side trips without which some of the most meaningful things are missed.

HOW TO USE THIS BOOK

The chapters of this book are based on arbitrary division of the Gold Country, but each section centers around at least one major town where you will find accommodations. Every section would take at least a full weekend to cover if you plan to do anything more than merely drive through the old towns. But as convenient as the divisions are from this standpoint, don't attach any historical or geographical importance to the lines that we have drawn, unless, of course, they happen to be county lines, too.

On the opening page of each chapter, you will find a small map—a greatly simplified version of the foldout map following page 32—which locates the general area in the Gold Country that is covered in the chapter. The

towns in each section are not discussed in any strict geographical order, but rather in the order you might encounter on a motoring trip driving from south to north. The routes followed are, of course, only representative of many you might want to plan.

There are plenty of comfortable up-to-date hotels and motels in the Gold Country. Some of the motels have swimming pools—happy discoveries in summer.

Although much privately owned land is fenced and posted, there are still a number of places where you may camp. You will find privately operated campgrounds open to the public at lower elevations and Forest Service campgrounds higher in the mountains.

WINTER IS A GOOD TIME TO GO

During the winter you might find it worthwhile to plan overnight stays in the mild climate of the Gold Country and "commute" to the snow, which is usually only a few miles up any of the trans-mountain highways.

If you can, plan to stay at one of the old hotels that are still open for guests. It's an excellent way to "soak up" a lot of pioneer atmosphere, and for many Gold Country travelers an overnight stay at one of the comfortable old hostelries is the high point of their trip.

If you stop at one of these venerable inns, ask to see the register. You'll see a lot of names right out of the history books. At night you may hear Tommyknockers in the walls or ceiling, but don't let them worry you. Unemployed now, they're the benevolent gremlins that came into this country with the Cornish and Welsh miners, and they had their hands full as long as there were men underground to protect and timbering to test. Their irregular tapping there so close to your pillow has no particular significance now; like a lot of other old-timers, they just like to keep busy. So they tap away at any functioning timbers they find handy—and they listen for flaws with their heads cocked aside in rapt and solemn judgment. Go to sleep, and let them work.

LA GRANGE . . immense tailing piles

HORNITOS . . Murieta's haunts

MARIPOSA . . oldest courthouse

COULTERVILLE . . pioneer monument

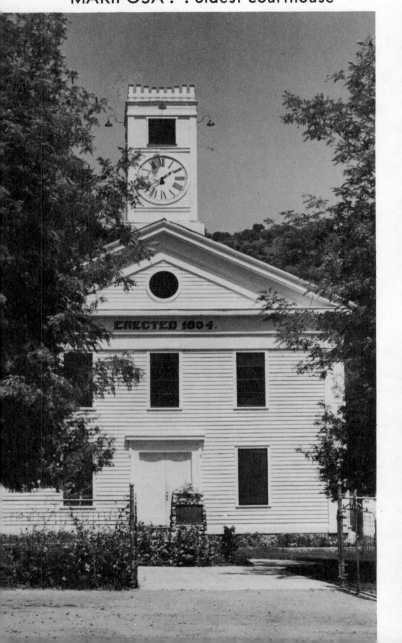

BAGBY . . originally "Ridley's Ferry"

Ben Hur to Coulterville

THE MARIPOSA AREA

MARIPOSA · MORMON BAR · BEN HUR · MOUNT BULLION

MOUNT OPHIR · HORNITOS · BEAR VALLEY · BAGBY

COULTERVILLE · LA GRANGE

Mariposa

Halfway along the 80-mile drive from Merced to Yosemite Valley on Highway 140 lies Mariposa, the southernmost town of major historical importance in the Mother Lode.

The town, which is built along the eastern side of a typical upper Sierra foothill valley, was part of the 46,000-acre tract belonging to John C. Fremont, famed explorer, soldier, and politician. His office building, one of several early brick structures still standing, is in use today.

The town's lovely name means "butterfly" in Spanish, and it was for the beautiful, fluttering masses of butterflies that are found in the area at certain times of the year that the town and the county for which it serves as county seat were named. Mariposa was an official seat of government for an area which reached from the foothills east to the Nevada-Utah border and south to Los Angeles County before California became a part of the United States.

Although Mariposa is anything but a ghost town now,

there are quite a few early buildings that are easily found on or just off the main street. Among them are the Schlageter Hotel, the Trabucco warehouse, the jail, the Fremont office, and the I.O.O.F. hall. But most visitors agree with Gold Country connoisseurs that the wooden court house with its stark white walls and classically simple lines on a rise at the north end of town is the most striking memento of the past. It has served as court house continuously since 1854, and the big clock in the tower has rung the hours since it was installed in 1866. Another old institution is the *Mariposa Gazette* which, like the court house, dates back to 1854.

It was from Mariposa in 1851 that Major James Savage led a battalion of volunteers in a search for the stronghold of marauding Indians who had periodically raided mining camps in the area. The fact that they caught and punished the red men has been all but forgotten. But through this action a gift of incredible beauty was

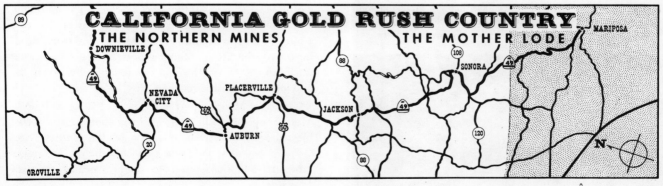

Between Cathay and Mormon Bar. Row of dead coyotes strung up by their "heels" on a barbed wire fence along Old Highway give a mute warning to fellow predators. This cunning animal is hunted by ranchers all through the Mother Lode Country

Mariposa. The Schlageter Hotel, which was built in the 1850's, looks down on the main highway through Mariposa. The brick structure with its delicate wooden balconies is characteristic of architectural style of the time. Note high sidewalks

Between Mount Bullion and Bear Valley. Here the road is narrow and quiet. The blue oaks which line the curving highway are found throughout the Mother Lode foothills. Digger pines and autumn-blooming tarweed are usually found with the oaks

given the world, for the Indians' mountain stronghold was magnificent Yosemite Valley.

Mormon Bar

Just two miles southeast of Mariposa is Mormon Bar, named for the Mormons who settled there in 1849. Although the Mormons moved on after a short stay, others moved in and the camp became a bustling, prosperous settlement in the 1850's as did Bootjack five miles to the east.

On the bank of nearby Mariposa Creek you can see ruins of old adobe buildings and the remains of a Chinese cemetery from whose ground friends and relatives dug bones of the dead to be carried back to China for final rest in ancestral burial grounds.

Ben Hur

Traveling south from Mormon Bar on the well-kept county road you will reach Ben Hur, the site of a mining camp of which little more than the name remains.

There is one well-preserved remainder of the early days, however—the remarkable stone wall which encircles the 4,000-acre Quick ranch. Built by Chinese coolies in 1862, the wall marches five miles across the rolling hills. While it was being built, each coolie was required to lay 25 feet of wall each day or lose his job. His pay for this staggering labor: 25 cents a day—a penny a foot.

Mount Bullion and Mount Ophir

When you travel north from Mariposa on a quiet, winding stretch of Highway 49, the first village you reach is Mount Bullion. As with so many town sites along Gold Country roads, there is little left to suggest the fevered activity of 2,000 men who first worked the placers, then turned to the rich quartz veins in their search for gold. The now vanished Princeton Mine, which produced more than $3,000,000, was once a property of John C. Fremont.

The Trabucco Store, one of several in Mariposa County, is still in use, and across the street are the weathered remains of the Marre Store. The building, with walls of foot-square adobe blocks, was built before 1860. Two miles beyond, the ruins of several stone buildings mark the site of Mount Ophir, once one of several camps in the Mount Bullion constellation but today the only one with visible remains.

It was at Mount Ophir in the early 1850's that John L. Moffatt operated the first private mint in California blessed with official authorization of the United States Government. The gold that went into the mint's famous octagonal $50 slugs was taken from a nearby claim of Moffatt's.

Mariposa. St. Joseph's Catholic Church, built in 1862, stands on a prominence above the south end of town. View of Mariposa and surroundings is excellent from this point. If you enter town on Highway 140 from the south, look to the right for the church

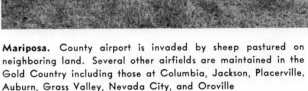

Mariposa. County airport is invaded by sheep pastured on neighboring land. Several other airfields are maintained in the Gold Country including those at Columbia, Jackson, Placerville, Auburn, Grass Valley, Nevada City, and Oroville

Hornitos

The 13-mile drive from Mount Bullion west to Hornitos is out of the way, but the reward is well worth the extra hour it will take on your journey. The many charming old buildings that frame the Mexican-style plaza and the history of this once roaring, lawless town make it one of the most interesting stops in the Mother Lode.

Founded by Mexican miners who had been "voted" out of neighboring Quartzburg by a law-and-order committee of Americans, Hornitos reflects Mexican influence more than any other settlement in the Gold Country.

The town's name means "little ovens" in Spanish after the little oven-shaped tombs that the first settlers built above the ground for their dead.

Joaquin Murieta was a visitor to this wild town, it is said, and with little effort you can find someone to point out the tunnel through which the Mother Lode's most famous bad man retreated from the fandango hall when circumstances grew too hot for him. Others have unromantically claimed that the tunnel was used to roll beer barrels from a stable to the basement of the dance hall. Today the building serves as the post office.

Other buildings to look for are the Wells Fargo office —now the Native Sons of the Golden West parlor, the Masonic Lodge, and the remains of the D. Ghirardelli Store. It was in this last building that the man who was to accumulate a fortune in chocolate began to build his business empire.

Hornitos' reputation for wildness has been enhanced by stories like that of the two dance hall girls who, with shawls wrapped around their left arms as shields, duelled with knives in the darkness of early morning and by the

Mariposa. This is the interior of California's oldest courthouse. Frame was built with dovetailed joints and is held together with locust pegs. Court was held in this room before the Civil War. See exterior view on page 12

Hornitos. Street is almost deserted on this hot, dry, summer day. White building on the left is the only one-story Masonic lodge in the Gold Country. Trees, farther down the street, mark the Mexican-style plaza around which the town was built

Mount Ophir. Ruins of Trabucco Store stand in the shadow of shaggy oaks. The schist structure was built in 1852. Remains of a private mint which coined octagonal $50 slugs here from 1850 to 1852 have all but disappeared

dawn lay dead from their bloody wounds. But the tragic tale of the Chinese, who in a moment of rage fired a pistol to frighten a tormenting white boy and by accident slightly wounded him, is one which few stories still told in the Gold Country can match.

The Chinese realized that his chances would be best if he headed for the hills, but he was soon caught by a posse and escorted to the little jail which still stands in Hornitos.

Angry miners realized that it would be difficult, if not impossible, to break into the vault-like building, so with grisly ingenuity they lured the pitiful prisoner to the cell's tiny window with the promise of tobacco, then seized him, threw a noose around his neck and, by violently jerking the rope, literally dashed his brains out against the stone wall.

Bear Valley

The 11-mile drive from Hornitos to Bear Valley is across country common to much of the Mother Lode foothills—

Hornitos. This old photograph shows oven-like graves which suggested the town's name to early settlers. Hornitos means "little ovens" in Spanish. Hornitos shows Mexican influence more strongly than any other Gold Country town

Hornitos. Stone ruin on the left is the Ghirardelli Store. Plaque was placed on the building by descendants. Building in the center is the present post office but was once a fandango hall Joaquin Murieta is said to have frequented

hot in the summer, covered with poor dry grass and drought-resistant oaks; lonely country save for scurrying ground squirrels, the crafty coyotes which you rarely see, and the constant song of insects.

The few buildings left in Bear Valley don't speak of the days when General Fremont ruled his empire from the beautiful mansion he built for his wife and children, nor of the 3,000 souls that made up the little city when local quartz was yielding gold in abundance. Gone is the famed Oso House, a pillared and balconied hostelry built by Fremont in 1850 of lumber brought around the Horn. This grand old frame building was the victim of a carelessly started fire in the 1930's. But the sagging frame structures and stone and adobe ruins that remain are quite photogenic. Look for the Bon Ton Saloon, the roofless jail, the Fremont Company Store, old ore wagons, the local I.O.O.F. hall and Trabucco Store, and the vestiges of Chinese adobes at the northeast end of town. Unfortunately, nothing remains to mark the Fremont mansion.

It was here that the "Bear Valley War" was held between Fremont's men and a group of claim jumpers in 1858. The "war" involved more than 100 men and was held in dead earnest. Not a single shot was fired, but it is believed that only the appearance of state forces kept the affair from becoming a tragic piece of early California history.

Bagby

Farther north on Highway 49, about six miles from Bear Valley at the bottom of a long and twisting grade, is Bagby, marking the northern boundary of Fremont's empire. The view from the top of the grade is spectacular and comes as a surprise because the grade up from Bear Valley is so gradual.

Bear Valley. Here beside the highway are two relics of mining operations at the turn of the century. The wagons were used to haul ore to Bagby from the Pine Tree Mine north of Bear Valley. This town was the center of Fremont's empire

Coulterville. Lying in a peaceful foothill setting, Coulterville is the main stop between Mariposa and Jamestown on Highway 49. Visible, left center, behind the roofless stone shell, is the three-story Jeffery Hotel. Stone shell was once a hotel, too

Coulterville. Black Angus cow with her white-faced calf wander freely next to two of Coulterville's tourist attractions. The little steam engine was used on the four-mile railroad between town and the Mary Harrison Mine. Large oak is local "Hangin' Tree"

Near Coulterville. Remains of the Mary Harrison Mine include the red brick furnace that was once part of a boiler house. The mine was opened in the 1860's and, until its abandonment in 1903, produced several hundreds of thousands in gold

The town's prominent ruin is Benton Mills, built by Fremont and named for his father-in-law, Senator Thomas Hart Benton. Fremont's regard for the older man is shown in his naming not only this property for him, but also Mount Bullion to the south. Benton's nickname in national politics was "Old Bullion" because of his long advocacy of hard money.

Coulterville

For a town that has been gutted by fire three times, Coulterville has a remarkable collection of remains—strong stone walls and iron doors, old adobes, and the fine old Jeffery Hotel.

Originally called Banderita, the town was finally dubbed Coulterville for the enterprising Yankee, George W. Coulter who set up store in a tent at the site in 1849. When Coulter arrived there was a sizeable Mexican and Chinese population, but as in many other camps and towns of the Mother Lode, friction between the incoming American miners and the Mexicans led to violence and

Bagby. This tiny settlement, which hugs the banks of the Merced River, is at the bottom of a spectacular grade from Bear Valley. The foundations of Fremont's Benton Mills can be seen next to the Highway 49 bridge on the near side of the river

Coulterville. There's still loose gold along the Gold Country's creeks, and if you want to try your hand at panning, there are several places where you can pay for the privilege. Many "snipers" still pan for dust and occasional nuggets

ultimate expulsion of the Spanish-speaking "furriners."

The Jeffery Hotel, which is the town's most imposing structure, is neither stately nor preposterous in appearance, but about halfway between. The building was converted by George Jeffery in 1870 from a Mexican structure of rock and adobe built in 1851. The old walls are three feet thick.

Across the street you will see a small steam engine shaded by a large oak—the "hangin' tree." The engine was used by the Mary Harrison Mine to haul ore along a stretch of track known as the world's crookedest railroad. To reach the ruins of this mine, drive south from town about a mile until you come to dead end road going off to the right. You will see the mine on the left a short distance down this road.

The last fire to sweep Coulterville indirectly caused the village's last and perhaps the country's shortest "Gold Rush." In 1899, the year of the last fire, rubble of a stone and adobe building that was razed after the conflagration was used to fill chuckholes in the street. Apparently unknown to anyone living was a secret cache of gold coins in the very walls being used for fill. No sooner than the first rain were several of these coins exposed by the running water and the rush was on. As the story goes, the town's populace turned out armed with shovels, picks, butcher knives, spoons, and other improbable mining tools, and quickly reduced the street to a state of impassable confusion—far worse than before repairs had been made.

La Grange

Not quite halfway between Modesto and Coulterville on the banks of the Tuolumne River, is the picturesque village of La Grange, only a vestige of the busy trading center it was in the 1850's. Settled by miners in 1852, it quickly adapted to a business role as the miners moved farther back into the hills in the search for gold. Mountains of water-smoothed rocks line the river's banks for miles as testimony to the incredible energy of early-day miners.

In the 1870's, $5,000,000 worth of ditches and flumes carried water for hydraulic mining, but since 1883, when the Anti-Debris Act was enacted, dredging has been the only mining activity in the area. Even today, dredges slowly work the river bottom above the town, piling behind them gigantic tailings that look, when seen from a distance, as though they might have been squeezed from a Gargantuan pastry tube.

A few stone and adobe buildings still stand, but it is hard to imagine the town, once called French Bar, as home for many hundreds, perhaps thousands.

East of La Grange. Although the foothills are hot and dry in summer, they turn green in spring. Here you see a bank of lupine, one of the many wildflowers that color the hills. The purple bloom of godetia is also a familiar sight

Western Mariposa County. Row after row of tailings left by dredges cover the landscape. Older piles in the upper half of the picture are overgrown with trees and brush. These piles are made up of rocks from fist to grapefruit size. (Air view)

COLUMBIA . . Fallon House Theater

"JIMTOWN" . . Gay Nineties style

CHINESE CAMP . . aged graveyard

ANGELS CAMP . old traction engine

NEAR YOSEMITE JUNCTION . ruins

KNIGHTS FERRY . . covered bridge

Second Garrote to Murphys

THE SONORA AREA

PRIESTS · BIG OAK FLAT · GROVELAND · SECOND GARROTE
JACKSONVILLE · CHINESE CAMP · KNIGHTS FERRY
COPPEROPOLIS · ALTAVILLE · ANGELS CAMP
CARSON HILL · MELONES · TUTTLETOWN · RAWHIDE
SHAWS FLAT · SPRINGFIELD · COLUMBIA · SONORA
JAMESTOWN · VALLECITO · DOUGLAS FLAT · MURPHYS

Priests and Big Oak Flat

If you turn off Highway 49 at Moccasin Creek Power House, you can take an hour's tour through several settlements that still preserve some of the flavor of pioneer days.

Near this turnoff, incidentally, is the Moccasin Creek State Fish Hatchery, where visitors are welcome.

The first community you'll reach is Priests, site of the famous Priest Hotel that served early travelers to Yosemite Valley and miners on their way to and from the mines. The hotel, with its excellent food and spectacular seven-county view, enjoyed world-wide fame, but fire long ago took the last remainder of the once-proud structure.

A mile farther up the grade, you will reach the little town that gives the road its name—Big Oak Flat.

The huge oak that inspired the name was killed in the fire of 1862. In 1869, the tree overturned as miners burrowed for gold in the ground on which it stood. There it lay until 1901, when fire destroyed it. Along Highway 120 at the original site, a piece of the tree is encased in a marker.

The gold-laden gravels which made Big Oak Flat a rich placer camp were discovered by James D. Savage in 1850. Savage was accompanied by five Indian wives and several Indian servants. It was Savage, you may recall, who later discovered Yosemite Valley when he commanded a group of volunteers in pursuit of marauding Indians.

Groveland

Groveland, two miles beyond Big Oak Flat, was originally called Garrote. The town serves as a supply center for the neighboring ranches and farms and the few small mines still in operation.

The name Groveland, which appeared officially in the 1870's, was chosen in quiet contrast to the original which was selected in 1850 to remind citizens of the hanging of a horse thief which took place there.

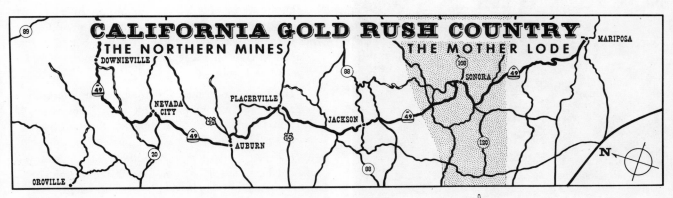

Second Garrote. Two-story house built by Chaffee and Chamberlain in 1853 is now called "Bret Harte Cabin." Most historians think that Bret Harte never came near Second Garrote, but the story persists that the author once lived here

Second Garrote. This massive trunk is all that remains of one of the Gold Country's "Hangin' Trees." The claim that 60 men were strung up from its branches is probably an exaggeration, however. The section of rope is a recent addition

The Wells Fargo office and the balconied Groveland Hotel are the town's most prominent reminders of the past.

Second Garrote

Second Garrote, which is about two miles beyond Groveland, is the site of a tenacious bit of lore that will probably never be substantiated. But the touching true story attached to it should be preserved.

Jason P. Chamberlain and James A. Chaffee were young men when they settled in Second Garrote in 1852. There they built a two-story frame house and lived as inseparable friends for the next 51 years. Long before Chaffee died in 1903, their reputation for loyalty to each other and kindness to travelers that passed on Big Oak Flat Road became a legend. Chamberlain lived on three months after Chaffee's death, but finally took his own life, heartbroken and lonely.

A bit of scholarly speculation by an English professor gave rise to the notion that these two men were models for the protagonists in Bret Harte's story, "Tennessee's Partner." Apparently, from this innocent academic inquiry, the story grew until the house was called "Bret Harte's Cabin" and a 25c admission was actually charged.

The house today bears a prominent sign reading "The Bret Harte Cabin," and you will find some who will repeat the story of Chamberlain and Chaffee and tell you positively that Harte developed his story from their lives. Unfortunately, there isn't a scrap of evidence to show that the Gold Country's most celebrated author ever came near the area, much less the "Bret Harte Cabin."

Jacksonville

Driving back down Priests Grade, you may catch a glimpse of the old stagecoach road on the other side of the canyon; and here, as on many other Gold Country roads, you will have little difficulty spotting several abandoned mines without leaving your car.

Once back on Highway 49, you can continue on down to Jacksonville, at one time a rival of Sonora and Columbia for eminence in the Southern Mines but today just a small village on the banks of the Tuolumne where Woods Creek joins it.

The town was named for Colonel Alden Jackson, a veteran of the war with Mexico, who discovered gold there in June of 1849. The bustling town of Jackson to the north also honors this early pioneer.

The first orchard in the Southern Mines area was planted here, and it has only been a few decades since the last remaining apple trees have disappeared.

Chinese Camp

Climbing on Highway 49 northwest of Jacksonville, you will travel from the rocky river bottom to broad, rolling foothills. Four miles from Jacksonville is Chinese Camp which sits like an oasis amid grass and tarweed fields. These fields, which are so characteristic of the western half of the Mother Lode region, turn a beautiful gold when the tarweed blooms in August, September, and October. Among the town's tree-shaded old structures are the Wells Fargo Express building, now in ruins, the post office, and Rosenblum's Store.

How the thousands of Chinese who mined in the area in the early 1850's arrived is still in doubt, but it was for them the town was named.

The second big tong war to be held in the state—the first was in Weaverville two years earlier—was fought near Chinese Camp over a century ago and it is a story worth repeating.

It all started when a huge stone rolled from the diggings of one group of Chinese to an area where another group was working. A fight ensued, and when it ended, the groups sent out a call for help to their respective tongs—the Sam Yap and the Yan Wo. Each group felt it had lost face and the only proper thing to do was to hold a full scale war between the tongs.

Preparations were hurriedly made, and each side built up an arsenal of crude iron weapons fashioned by American blacksmiths for the purpose—pikes, spears, daggers, and the like. A few firearms were brought from San Francisco, and Yankee miners were hired to instruct the combatants in the use of these instruments of destruction —strange to the Chinese.

Finally, on October 25, 1856, twelve hundred members of the Sam Yap fraternity met nine hundred Yan Wo tong brothers in the famous "Chinese War." The battle

Moccasin Creek. Here is a view of the Moccasin Creek Power House showing the four parallel penstocks that carry the water needed to turn the turbines. Nearby is the Moccasin Creek Fish Hatchery, which is open to the public

Big Oak Flat. Typical old Mother Lode building of dressed stone and brick with characteristic iron doors intact. Big Oak Flat, originally called Savage Diggings after James Savage, camp's founder, was once center for several productive mines

Between Moccasin Creek and Jacksonville. This roughly built shrine, long since abandoned to the weather, stands at the side of Highway 49. The once-stuccoed structure was probably built by devout Italian immigrants after the Gold Rush

Tuolumne River. This is one of the main rivers that cut across the Gold Country. It joins Woods Creek at Jacksonville about two miles west of this point. The river is dammed far above in Yosemite National Park to form Hetch Hetchy Reservoir

was fought on Crimea Flat, which is about 3 miles from Chinese Camp.

When the smoke cleared, and the gladiators had left the battlefield—some voluntarily, another 250 as prisoners of American law authorities—the casualties were totaled: Four dead and four injured.

Amidst the ruins in the village, you will notice a locust-like tree growing in profusion. This is the Chinese tree of heaven which was planted by the Chinese wherever they settled in the Gold Country. When you see a clump of these trees growing by the road, it is quite possible that Chinese lived somewhere near years ago.

American pioneers were partial to the fig, apple, pear, elm, and locust, and if you find an old specimen of one of these growing, in all probability a cabin once stood nearby even if no other sign of habitation exists.

Knights Ferry

Unless you are traveling east from Oakdale to the Gold Country, you will have to turn west at Yosemite Junction

Jacksonville. The village sits at the base of the gorge where Woods Creek and the Tuolumne River meet. The road leading north to Stent from which this picture was taken winds up through steep mountain country to Jamestown

on Highway 120 to see Knights Ferry—off the well-traveled track, but with several points of interest important to Gold Country *aficianados.*

The town was settled in spring of 1849 by William Knight, who six years earlier had founded Knights Landing north of Sacramento.

John and Lewis Dent acquired the town's profitable ferry in the winter of 1849 after the death of Knight and later built a grist mill and sawmill downstream from the long covered bridge which crosses the Stanislaus River just above town. This bridge was built in the 1860's by Lewis Dent to replace a similar one designed by his brother-in-law, U. S. Grant, who later became 18th president of the United States.

Grant, who was married to Julia Dent, visited Knights Ferry in 1854, and townspeople can point out for you the old Dent house where he stayed during his visit. The weathered old frame building is still occupied.

The first bridge was washed away in 1862, but the present bridge is identical to it—and eight feet higher. Imposing ruins of the grist mill which was built to replace the original one that was washed away in the same flood can be seen from both sides of the river.

Look also for the solid iron jail on the north side of the road after you pass the grist mill going into town, and beyond that the old fire house and Masonic Building.

Copperopolis

A mile below Yosemite Junction, a country road leads west to Copperopolis from which you can get a sweeping view of fabled Table Mountain. You'll cross the Stanislaus River on a new bridge, but for almost a century travelers drove through a covered bridge at O'Byrnes Ferry, a site now covered by water behind Tulloch Dam. Crossing the

Knights Ferry. View toward the covered bridge from the foundations of a grist mill built in the 1850's. Original bridge and mill were lost in the flood of 1862. The driftwood you see here accumulated in the disastrous flood of 1956

Chinese Camp. This town is only four miles from Jacksonville, but the surrounding country is radically different. In the foreground is an old stone building with a false front. The trees growing about it are Chinese trees of heaven

Chinese Camp. The post office was built in the 1850's and is still in use. Placer mining was carried on here with water brought in by flume and ditch from Woods Creek. Another old building still used is the St. Francis Xavier Catholic Church

Knights Ferry. This is the Dent house, built in the early 1850's, where U. S. Grant stayed during his 1854 visit. Tall locusts shade the still-occupied residence. John and Lewis Dent, who bought original ferry, were brothers of Julia Dent, Grant's wife

Knights Ferry. This handsome monument, erected by the Daughters of the American Revolution, stands on the banks of the Stanislaus River. Markers like this can be found all over the Gold Country, and the list of sponsoring organizations is growing

Knights Ferry. This bizarre gravestone reads:
"Erectet by William Walther to the memory of Katherine Walther born the 1 of August 1852 born dukedom of Nassau killed the 1 of June 1860 by a Mesican"

bridge, you'll circle the base of Table Mountain and pass mile after mile of stone fence.

Copperopolis, which is 13 miles from Highway 120, was founded prior to the War Between the States. It is something of an oddity and perhaps a little out of place in a story of the Gold Country. The town was and perhaps may again be an important copper producing center but it never knew prosperity as a gold camp. There is no mining going on today, but at one time the area was the most important copper ore producer in the United States.

In the early days of the mines' operation, ore was carried by cart to Stockton, then by river boat to San Francisco Bay where it was loaded onto sailing ships for the long trip around Cape Horn to Wales for smelting.

Some of the buildings which still stand here were built in the 1860's of brick hauled from Columbia where buildings were being torn down by miners to get at the gold-rich soil on which that town was built.

At the south end of town across from the junction with Highway 4, there are three buildings, obviously old. The biggest, a brick structure with huge iron shutters and doors, was once the Federal Armory. The building was headquarters for Union troops during the Civil War. Next to it are the old warehouse and office buildings of the Copper Consolidated Mining Company whose headframes and tailing piles are visible across the street.

At the other end of town, on the uphill side of the road, is the I.O.O.F. hall—originally a church and recently used as a community center.

On Highway 4 west of Copperopolis, you will see a long stretch of stone fence. Townsfolk will tell you that it was perhaps built by Chinese or Chileans, but the favorite story (and the least probable) is that it was built

by persons of unknown nationality for three barrels of whiskey. Actually most of the many miles of stone fence were built by James Sykes, a resident of now-vanished Telegraph City.

Altaville

Twelve miles north and east of Copperopolis at the junction of Highways 4 and 49 is Altaville, first known as Cherokee Flat and as Forks In The Road.

Halfway between the towns, you will come across a pair of early stone corrals, but other than that and the remains of a few small mines, there is little sign of pioneer activity along the road.

On the west side of Highway 49 in Altaville, you'll find the handsome old Prince and Garibardi Store—a well preserved two-story stone building erected over a century ago.

Altaville's name will probably be remembered because it was the starting place of what is today considered by many as the Gold Country's greatest hoax. It was from deep in a mine in nearby Bald Mountain that a human skull—soon to be known to the world as the Pliocene Skull—was taken in 1866 and presented to the scientific world as the remains of a prehistoric man. The argument over authenticity of the skull continued for almost half a century, and even today not all authorities can agree.

Bret Harte's poem "To the Pliocene Skull," which captures the ridiculous aspects of the whole affair, suggests the horse laughter that must have filled many a miner's cabin.

True to the massive scale in which the joke was conceived, no one connected with the "crime" ever revealed his part. All who had anything to do with it are surely dead, and the truth will never be known.

Angels Camp

The first thing most people think of when they hear the name of this busy town is Mark Twain's wonderful story called "The Celebrated Jumping Frog of Calaveras

Copperopolis. Massive iron doors on the old armory at the right may be the largest in the Gold Country. On the day Lincoln died, Union soldiers marched from here to the church at the north end of town for services. Mine warehouse is next door

County." The story was set in Angels Camp, and the town will never let the world forget it. There is one statue of a frog and another of Twain, and every year in May the International Frog Olympics are held here to celebrate the first and most famous contest.

Copperopolis. Headframe of the Copper Consolidated Mining Company's Union shaft towers over forlorn shell of an old mine building. The area was once the greatest copper center in the country, but no ore has been mined here for years

Copperopolis. 1866 headstone in the old graveyard on the hill southeast of town reads:

"Stop traveler, and cast an eye.
As you are now, so once was I."

Copperopolis. Stately brick structure was originally a church. It was in this building that memorial services for Lincoln were held. Later it was used as the Odd Fellows Hall. It stands on a hillside east of the road at north end of town

In addition to this lively bit of history, the town has several old buildings that were built in the 1850's, including the Peirano Building and the Angels Hotel.

Residential sections visible from the highway have a particular charm that only well kept old homes can impart. Although the placers gave out quickly, the discovery of gold-bearing quartz established Angels Camp

Between Altaville and Copperopolis. This stone corral is one of a pair which straddles the road halfway between the towns. Many miles of stone fencing built long ago can be seen through the foothills in the Mother Lode Country

as an important mining center—a role it kept for decades.

The discovery of the quartz lode came about in a curious way. A miner named Raspberry, for whom Raspberry Lane—still a public way in Angels Camp—was named, was having difficulty with his muzzle-loading rifle one day. The ramrod had jammed and in a moment of exasperation he fired the rifle into the ground. The ramrod shot out and struck the ground with force. When he went to retrieve the rod, he found a piece of rock which had broken from the impact and glittered with what was unmistakably gold. Raspberry took almost $10,000 from the new claim in three days and went on to make a fortune following the vein.

Carson Hill

On the highway between Angels Camp and Carson Hill sits a large and lonely stone and adobe house slowly falling to pieces. This stretch of road was once crowded with buildings, but only this structure, the Romaggi adobe, remains to mark the settlement of Albany Flat.

James Romaggi arrived from Genoa in 1850 and scorning gold, he built this house and planted vineyards and orchards to establish one of the finest ranches in the Mother Lode. Drought long ago killed the vines and trees, but even in parched surroundings, the house is a beautiful sight.

A few buildings, mostly frame construction, without historical importance and with little individual character, comprise the present settlement of Carson Hill. But in its heyday, Carson Hill was considered the richest of all the rich Mother Lode camps.

The town was named for James Carson, a miner who traveled to the region with George Angel, for whom Angels Camp was named, and the Murphy brothers, John and Daniel, who founded Murphys to the north.

Going south through the village you can see the yawning opening of the Morgan Mine on the hill above town. Fifteen miles of tunnel run through the hill, and one of the shafts reaches down almost 5,000 feet.

It was in Carson Hill that the nation's largest nugget was found. The massive piece of gold weighed 195 pounds and was valued at $73,710.

Melones

Practically nothing remains of the Stanislaus River camp, named by the Spanish-speaking miners for the coarse nuggets resembling melon seeds that were found there.

Ruins of the Vignoli Trading Post and a Mexican adobe which dates back to 1849 are all that is left of the wild camp of the 1850's.

The town, which was once called Slumgullion by Yankee miners, was the site of Robinson's Ferry which, it is claimed, took in over $10,000 in a period of six weeks during the peak of the Rush.

Tuttletown

If you travel farther south on Highway 49, you pass the markers pointing to the Mark Twain Cabin on Jackass Hill. The cabin is a reconstruction built around the fireplace of the Gillis brothers' cabin where Twain was a guest for several months. It was during this visit that he heard the original tale on which he based "The Celebrated Jumping Frog of Calaveras County."

Altaville. Prince and Garibardi Store built of dressed stone stands on the west side of Highway 49 in the center of town. Close by is the D. D. Demarest Foundry—oldest iron works in continuous operation in California

Jackass Hill was a rich placer mining area and was on a pack route over which the braying animals that gave the camp its name trudged in great numbers.

A mile beyond the Jackass Hill turnoff you'll come to what was once Tuttletown—today it's not even a wide place on the winding highway. The remains of a rapidly disintegrating stone building—Swerer's Store—is all one can find of the once-prosperous camp. The town was

Altaville. This brick schoolhouse served the town from 1858 until 1950. Plaque tells that funds to build the structure were raised at a dance. The building is now located on the grounds of the State Highway Maintenance Station

Angels Camp. Highway 49 curves through this famous Mother Lode town. High sidewalks follow contour of the hillside as it was before smooth road was built. False fronts and galvanized iron roofs can be seen all through the Gold Country

named for Judge Anson Tuttle who built the first permanent house in Tuolumne County on the site in 1848.

Rawhide

Halfway along the short cut from Tuttletown to Jamestown, lies Rawhide, as quiet an inhabited town as you'll find in all the Gold Country. This little farming community, sitting under the glowering brow of Table Mountain, gives no hint that it was the location of the Rawhide Quartz Mine, once considered one of the world's great

Angels Camp. Fishing in the Gold Country varies, but the cold running mountain streams are ideally suited to trout. Feeder streams and lakes higher in the Sierra are usually better than the rivers at lower levels, but don't try to convince these lads

gold mines. The operation produced over $6,000,000 up to 1909.

Shaws Flat and Springfield

A little more than two miles from Sonora on Highway 49 northeast of the Rawhide turnoff is a crossroad, one branch of which leads to Shaws Flat and Sonora and the other to Springfield and Columbia.

Shaws Flat, which lies in a meadow with a skyline dominated by rows of Lombardy poplars, was the starting place in the career of James G. Fair who went on to amass a fortune in the Comstock Rush.

The old Mississippi House, which was built in 1851, still stands, but nothing remains of the bar that stood across the street, except a fine Gold Country story.

It was at this bar, it is said, that an enterprising bartender supplemented his daily wages in a particularly imaginative way. It seems that he would drop on the bar a wee bit of each pinch of dust that he took from the miners' pokes for their drinks. Now this took slight imagination, but the ingenious part of the larceny lay in his method of recovery.

Periodically leaving the bar to tramp around in the mud made by a little spring behind the building, he would return to his station and carefully pick up with his muddy boots all the gold dust he had dropped and carefully brushed to the floor. Then at night he panned out the mud scraped from his boots—and rich diggings they were. According to the story, he averaged about $30 a night during the week, and several times that on the weekends.

Angels Camp. This statue of Mark Twain stands in a small park in the center of town right on Highway 49. Twain's immortal story, "The Celebrated Jumping Frog of Calaveras County," vaulted him to prominence and put the town on the map

Angels Camp. Giant bits cut this core out of solid rock to drive a shaft deeper into the earth in the search for gold-bearing quartz. Since hydraulic mining was halted in 1884, hardrock mines have been the state's main producers

Angels Camp. It's only logical that a monument should have been raised to the frog. Every year in May, the town honors the famous frog of Twain's tale by holding the International Frog Olympics—the world's best known frog jumping contest

Springfield, which was named for a prodigious spring which gushes forth from between limestone boulders and is the source of Mormon Creek, was originally laid out on a plaza, but today only one old structure is left. The tree-shaded building, located on the north side of the Columbia road, was originally built as a church but was converted for military use at the beginning of the Civil War.

Columbia

Surrounded by hundreds of acres of exposed limestone washed clean of fabulously rich red clay by hydraulic Monitors, sits Columbia, "Gem of the Southern Mines."

This town, which was, and in one sense still is, one of the most important settlements in the Mother Lode, is today maintained as a state park.

Many brick buildings, most of which were built in the 1850's after fire had destroyed earlier frame buildings, line several shaded streets, and the town's claim of being the best preserved in the Gold Country cannot be disputed.

Originally called Hildreths Diggings and American Camp, Columbia was one of the richest of all the Gold Rush towns. It's a little difficult to imagine the quiet streets and aged buildings ringing with the clamor of thousands of miners, gamblers, merchants, dance hall girls, and miscellaneous camp followers that made up the hardy community. But like most robust towns of the early days—Mokelumne Hill, Sonora, Hornitos, Melones, among others—the boisterous era was short, and it mellowed as have the rest.

But the climax to mob violence didn't come until 1855 when Columbians participated in the Gold Country's most shockingly ugly lynching—an event which so deeply affected the conscience of the times that it can be called a turning point in the civilizing process which was to turn

(continued on page 38)

TYPICAL MOTORIST'S VIEW ... Highway 49 near Carson Hill

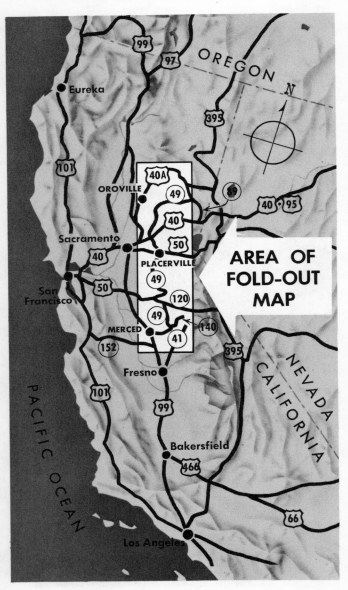

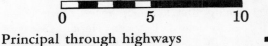

GOLD RUSH COUNTRY MAP

On the five-page foldout map that follows, you see the Gold Rush Country—crossed by seven trans-Sierra highways (U. S. 40, U. S. 50, State 88, 4, 108, 120, 140), traced lengthwise by State Highway 49, and subtly patterned with a fascinating network of back roads. For the approaches from the Northwest, the San Francisco Bay area, Southern California, the Mountain States, and the Southwest, see the locator map to the left.

Notice how many ways you can include a portion of the Gold Country in almost any cross-Sierra or north-south trip.

At the opening of each chapter you will find a greatly reduced and simplified version of this five-page map, and on each of the little maps there is a shaded area that corresponds to the area covered in the text that follows. For details of each area, refer back to the appropriate section of this big map.

Principal through highways

Secondary highways

Main local roads (oil or gravel surface)

Minor roads (rough, dusty, or muddy)

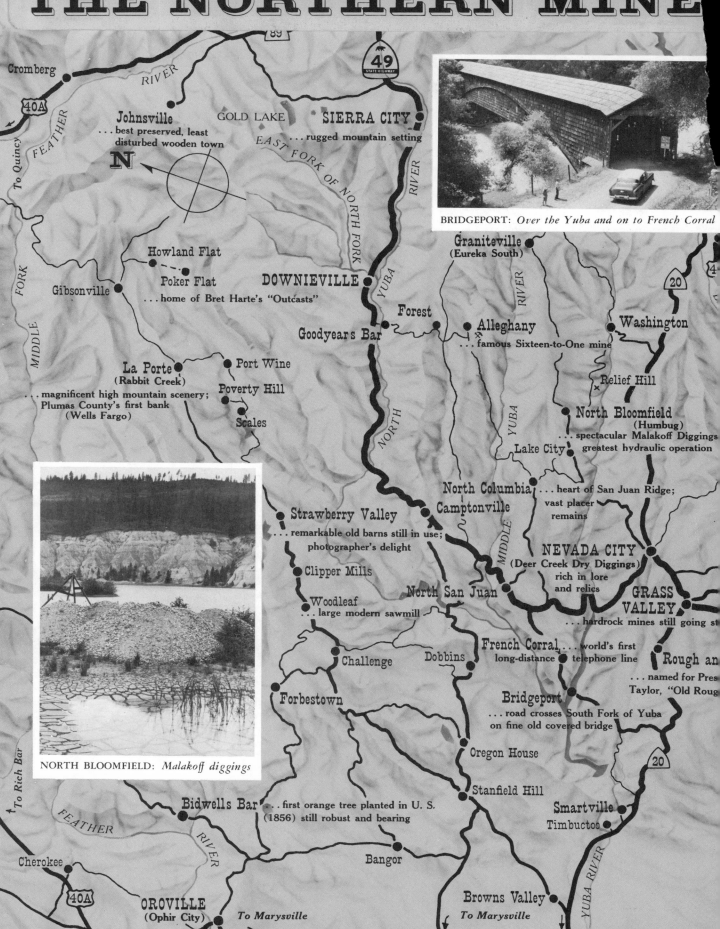

To Truckee

89

49 STATE HIGHWAY

Cromberg
40A
To Quincy

Johnsville
. . . best preserved, least disturbed wooden town

GOLD LAKE

SIERRA CITY
. . . rugged mountain setting

N

FEATHER RIVER

EAST FORK OF NORTH FORK

RIVER

BRIDGEPORT: *Over the Yuba and on to French Corral*

Howland Flat

Poker Flat

Gibsonville

DOWNIEVILLE
. . . home of Bret Harte's "Outcasts"

Graniteville
(Eureka South)

20

4

Forest

Goodyears Bar

Alleghany
. . . famous Sixteen-to-One mine

Washington

RIVER

YUBA

La Porte
(Rabbit Creek)

Port Wine

Poverty Hill

Scales

. . . magnificent high mountain scenery;
Plumas County's first bank
(Wells Fargo)

Relief Hill

North Bloomfield
(Humbug)
. . . spectacular Malakoff Diggings
greatest hydraulic operation

Lake City

NORTH

YUBA

MIDDLE FORK

NORTH BLOOMFIELD: *Malakoff diggings*

North Columbia

Camptonville

. . . heart of San Juan Ridge;
vast placer
remains

Strawberry Valley
. . . remarkable old barns still in use;
photographer's delight

NEVADA CITY
(Deer Creek Dry Diggings)
rich in lore
and relics

MIDDLE

Clipper Mills

Woodleaf
. . . large modern sawmill

North San Juan

GRASS
VALLEY
. . . hardrock mines still going st

French Corral . . . world's first
long-distance telephone line

Rough an
. . . named for Pres
Taylor, "Old Roug

Challenge

Dobbins

Forbestown

Bridgeport
. . . road crosses South Fork of Yuba
on fine old covered bridge

20

Oregon House

To Rich Bar

Stanfield Hill

Bidwells Bar . . . first orange tree planted in U. S.
(1856) still robust and bearing

Smartville

Timbuctoo

FEATHER RIVER

Bangor

Cherokee

40A

OROVILLE
(Ophir City)

To Marysville

Browns Valley

To Marysville

YUBA RIVER

To Sonora Pass

ODE

COLUMBIA: *Best preserved gold town*

FOOTHILLS: *Blue oaks, Digger pine, tarweed*

108

Twain Harte

Tuolumne
... terminus of Sierra Railroad

120

Second Garrote

Groveland
(Garrote)

COULTERVILLE
(Banderita)

Soulsbyville

Priests

Big Oak Flat

4

Sheep Ranch

Yankee Hill

Sawmill Flat
Squabbletown

SONORA

Moccasin Creek
... big power house; fish
hatchery you can visit

COLUMBIA
(American Camp)

MURPHYS
... well preserved,
tree-shaded

Springfield

Shaws Flat

JAMESTOWN

Douglas Flat

Vallecito

Tuttletown

Jacksonville

anch

Jackass Hill

Rawhide

Stent

120

Roaring Camp

Woods Crossing

Carson Hill

CHINESE CAMP

Calaveritas
eautiful drive from
9; sleepy, pastoral

Melones (Slumgullion)
... gold resembled melon seeds

49
STATE HIGHWAY

Altaville
(Cherokee Flat)

ANGELS CAMP
... Mark Twain's Jumping Frog
jumped here

Yosemite
Junction

132

E HILL
uilding

49
STATE HIGHWAY

LA GRANGE
... miles of patterned
"diggings" left by dredges

.ch

SAN ANDREAS

ave been "Chile Gulch"
—worked by Chilean miners

Copperopolis

120

Valley Springs

KNIGHTS FERRY
... ruins of big grist mill;
long covered bridge

4

Burson

Jenny Lind
Jenny Lind never
got within 2,000 miles

KNIGHT'S FERRY: *History on gravestones*

8

To Stockton

To Manteca

OAKDALE

To Modesto

CATTLE DRIVES *from summer pasture in the Sierra*

MURPHYS *grammar school built in 1860*

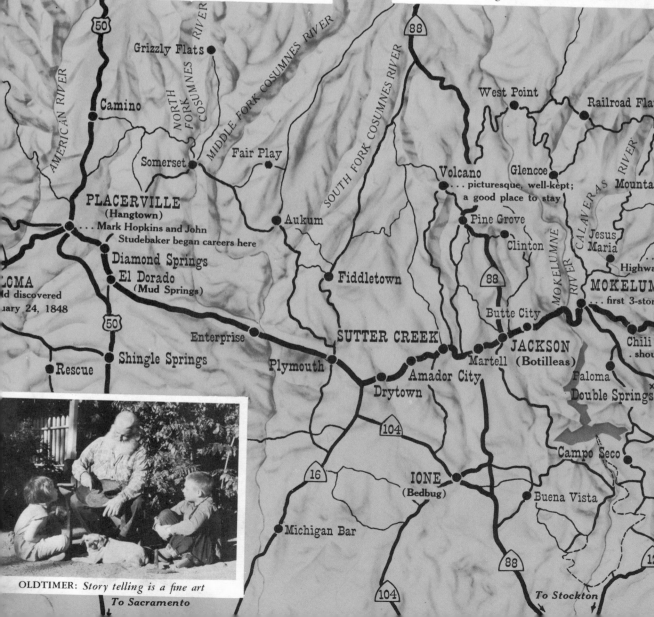

50

Grizzly Flats

Camino

NORTH FORK COSUMNES RIVER

MIDDLE FORK COSUMNES RIVER

Somerset   Fair Play

AMERICAN RIVER

PLACERVILLE
(Hangtown)
. . . Mark Hopkins and John
Studebaker began careers here

Diamond Springs
El Dorado
(Mud Springs)

LOMA
ld discovered
uary 24, 1848

50

Enterprise

Rescue   Shingle Springs

Aukum

SOUTH FORK COSUMNES RIVER

Fiddletown

Plymouth

Drytown

Amador City

SUTTER CREEK

104

16

Michigan Bar

88

West Point

Railroad Flat

Volcano
. . . picturesque, well-kept;
a good place to stay

Glencoe   Mountain

Pine Grove

Clinton

88

Jesus
Maria

CALAVERAS RIVER

. . . b
Highway

MOKELUMN
. . . first 3-story b

MOKELUMNE RIVER

Butte City

JACKSON
(Botilleas)

Martell

Chili Gu
. should

Paloma

Double Springs

Campo Seco

IONE
(Bedbug)

Buena Vista

88

12

OLDTIMER: *Story telling is a fine art*
To Sacramento

104   To Stockton

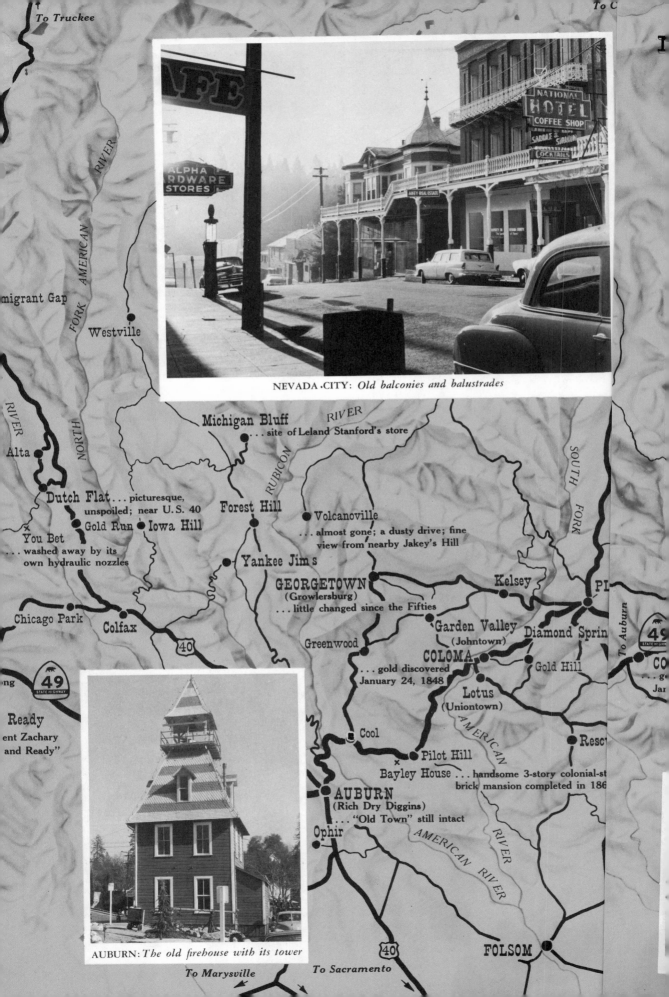

To Truckee

To C

migrant Gap

RIVER

Westville

NORTH FORK AMERICAN RIVER

Alta

Dutch Flat... *picturesque, unspoiled; near U.S. 40*

Gold Run • Iowa Hill

You Bet
... *washed away by its own hydraulic nozzles*

Chicago Park   Colfax

40

ng

49
STATE HIGHWAY

Ready
ent Zachary
and Ready"

NEVADA•CITY: *Old balconies and balustrades*

Michigan Bluff   RIVER
... *site of Leland Stanford's store*

RUBICON RIVER

Forest Hill

Volcanoville
... *almost gone; a dusty drive; fine view from nearby Jakey's Hill*

Yankee Jims

GEORGETOWN
(Growlersburg)
... *little changed since the Fifties*

Greenwood

Kelsey   Pl

Garden Valley
(Johntown)

Diamond Sprin

SOUTH FORK

To Auburn

49
STATE HIGHWAY

CO
g
Jar

COLOMA
... *gold discovered January 24, 1848*

Gold Hill

Lotus
(Uniontown)

Resc

AMERICAN

Cool

Pilot Hill

Bayley House ... *handsome 3-story colonial-st brick mansion completed in 186*

AUBURN
(Rich Dry Diggins)
... *"Old Town" still intact*

Ophir

AMERICAN RIVER

AUBURN: *The old firehouse with its tower*

40

FOLSOM

To Marysville   To Sacramento

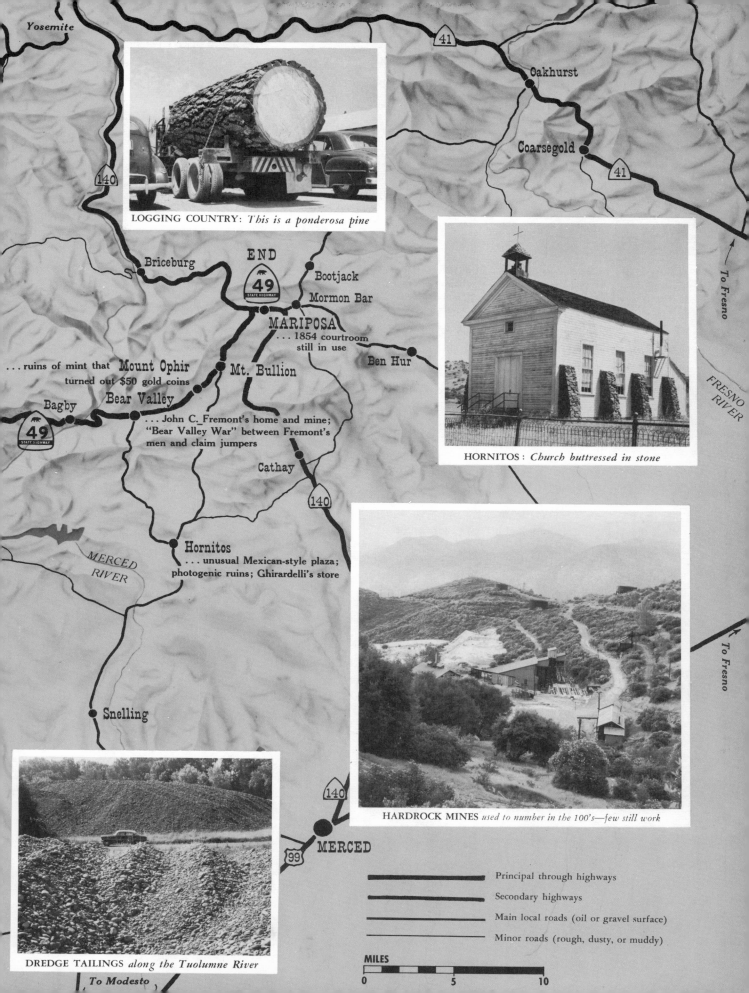

Yosemite

41

Oakhurst

Coarsegold

41

To Fresno

LOGGING COUNTRY: *This is a ponderosa pine*

140

Briceburg

END
49
STATE HIGHWAY

Bootjack

Mormon Bar

MARIPOSA

... 1854 courtroom
still in use

Ben Hur

... ruins of mint that
turned out $50 gold coins

Mount Ophir

Mt. Bullion

Bagby

Bear Valley

... John C. Fremont's home and mine;
"Bear Valley War" between Fremont's
men and claim jumpers

49
STATE HIGHWAY

Cathay

140

Hornitos

... unusual Mexican-style plaza;
photogenic ruins; Ghirardelli's store

*MERCED
RIVER*

FRESNO
RIVER

HORNITOS: *Church buttressed in stone*

To Fresno

Snelling

HARDROCK MINES *used to number in the 100's—few still work*

140

MERCED

99

DREDGE TAILINGS *along the Tuolumne River*

To Modesto

———————— Principal through highways

———————— Secondary highways

———————— Main local roads (oil or gravel surface)

———————— Minor roads (rough, dusty, or muddy)

MILES

0   5   10

Shaws Flat. Pastoral scene gives no hint of the great activity in the area after gold-bearing gravel was discovered under the thin lava surface. One claim yielded more than $250,000, and the discovery led to mining under Table Mountain

Near Carson Hill. The Romaggi ranch house, which is shown in a close-up view, is all that's left of Albany Flat. The building, with schist walls and locust lintels, is considered one of the most complex structures of its type and era

the wild camps into mature towns. Briefly, the circumstances were as follows:

A townsman named John Huron Smith weaved into a bar owned by Martha Barclay on one October afternoon and called for a drink. Mr. Smith was in no need of a drink, and in no time an argument broke out between him and Martha, a woman whose personal reputation matched that of her establishment—bad. Her swearing, apparently, caused Smith to push Martha and slap her in rage. Just as he did, Martha's new husband, John Barclay, appeared at the door, saw what was happening, and in an instant had drawn his pistol and killed his wife's tormentor.

It might have all been forgotten as a justifiable act, but the Barclays' name was unloved and Smith happened to be a good friend of State Senator J. W. Coffroth, an accomplished orator. Coffroth had no intention of letting the matter die, and he succeeded in warming a mob to lynch heat. They stormed the jail where Barclay was held and, overcoming the guard, took the terrified prisoner

Carson Hill. This camp is considered by many to have been the richest in all the Gold Country. A nugget worth over $73,000 was taken from the Morgan Mine whose "Glory Hole" can be seen on the mountain in the background

down the Gold Springs road to a great flume which towered 40 feet over the crowd. Kangaroo Court was quickly assembled, and it was obvious that only one verdict could be delivered, but before the "jury" returned from their deliberation, the sheriff arrived and attempted to take the prisoner from the mob. The sheriff was swamped by the mob, which then swept Barclay beneath the flume where a hastily tied noose was put around his neck. The rope was thrown over the flume and the howling mob watched a dozen men jerk the unfortunate man into the air.

But there were no cheers, for there by flickering torch light they saw in horror their victim hanging onto the rope above his head—in their frantic rush to have justice, no one had thought to tie his hands.

They quickly jerked the rope up and down, but still Barclay held fast—as long as he could keep the rope slack he would live. Then several of the lynchers clambered up the flume supports to shake the rope, but to no avail. Finally, tradition has it, one miner crawled out and with a pistol mercilessly battered Barclay's fists. He dropped, and with a final convulsive kick, died.

But the town had a fine side, too. Indeed, lawlessness was actually the exception, and what remains of Columbia is testimony to the honest energy of the town's early citizens.

In 1856, St. Anne's Roman Catholic Church was finished, and although it required restoration work in 1926, it has stood on Kennebec Hill at the west end of town for over a century. The church, considered one of the loveliest houses of worship in the Gold Country, was built by money contributed by miners.

The altar mural, painted by James Fallon, sign-painter

Tuttletown. This was Swerer's Store in 1932, but time has taken its toll. (Side view of same building, right, taken in 1956.) Mark Twain bought his supplies here when he stayed with the Gillis brothers at Jackass Hill

Tuttletown. This wall and the fallen iron doors are all that is left of Swerer's Store today. The remains can be seen right next to the winding highway. Ubiquitous Chinese trees of heaven, foreground, may soon overgrow the ruin

son of a local hotel keeper, is a loving work of art and an important point of interest.

Among the other buildings that you will find—and they are all marked for easy identification—are the Fallon House, an early-day hotel now used by the University of the Pacific as a summer theater; the Wells Fargo Express office, perhaps the most famous building in the Gold Country; the Stage Driver's Retreat; the D. O. Mills Bank; and the Masonic and Odd Fellows halls.

A trip to Columbia is a must if you visit the Mother Lode.

Sonora

Sonora was settled by Mexican miners two years before Columbia, but in the early 1850's the two towns battled it out for pre-eminence. Today there is no question about which is the liveliest—Sonora is booming still. As seat of Tuolumne County and a trading center for the surrounding cattle and lumber country, Sonora is as bustling as it was a century ago.

Springfield. This old building once stood on a large plaza with many other buildings, but now it ages away by itself. It was originally built as a church, but was used as an armory during the Civil War, and later as a school

Near Springfield. Limestone bedrock is now covered with growth, but in the 1850's the land was laid bare by hydraulicking. As an 1874 book described it, " . . . the miners searched, scraped and polished [the rocks] as a dentist does the teeth of his patient."

WEEKDAY AFTERNOON SCENE IN COLUMBIA

Columbia. You can see St. Anne's Church on a rise east of the Sonora road just before you reach Columbia. Columnar Italian cypresses stand before the entrance and look down on time-softened limestone bedrock that once held gold-bearing soil

Modern facades cover the aged buildings which line Washington Street and traffic moves slowly along the crowded thoroughfare. But even with its modern face, much in Sonora is left from the old days. Just drive off the main street half a block, and you'll find yourself passing from one century to another. Drive down Stewart Street, for instance, and look at the rear of Washington Street's buildings. Stewart is a block east of and parallel with Washington.

Unquestionably, the outstanding piece of old architecture in Sonora is St. James Episcopal Church, which stands at the head of Washington Street on the north end of town. This graceful frame structure was built in 1860, less than ten years after the shameful, but fortunately bloodless, "war" between Americans and the Mexican and Chilean miners of the town.

A vindictive $20 a month tax on foreigners, aimed principally at Mexican miners, caused the latter to band together in defiance. Although there was scattered violence, the Mexicans knew they were beaten, for the time being, and left the town in a mass exodus. Sonora's population dropped from 5,000 to 3,000 and the business community was on hard times until the tax was repealed in 1851 and Mexicans once again felt safe to return to Tuolumne County.

There are many stories about the "Queen of the Southern Mines," two of which are among the best the Gold Country has to offer.

One is the story of the Mexican and his three Indian companions who were found by American miners burning the corpses of two Americans. It took little time once

Sonora learned of the act for Judge Lynch to enter the story. But before the proceedings reached the point of no return, the prisoners were rescued just in time by an armed sheriff's posse from the mob which, so the story goes, already had the Mexican off the ground.

The town was sullen and rumors spread that a band of guerillas were stationed outside town waiting to sweep in to rescue the prisoners. The sheriff responded to this by rounding up over a hundred Mexicans, most of whom had just arrived in the area, on suspicion of murder. These prisoners were held in a corral to await examination after trial of the Mexican and his Indian friends.

Tension mounted and the town was swollen with hundreds of miners who had come for the trial. Just as court was about to convene, an accidental shot sparked a pandemonious outbreak of gunplay and only by some miracle was bloodshed averted.

The trial began, and the miners, whose tempers had been somewhat dampened by the wild outburst of shooting, must have felt even more sheepish—perhaps even ashamed—when the truth about the burning of the bodies was revealed: the Mexican and the three Indians were guilty of nothing more than committing an act of simple charity. They had discovered the murdered bodies of men they had never seen before, and, taking time out from their search for gold, had built funeral pyres in accordance with their religious belief.

Once the men were freed, the judge turned to examination of the hundred-odd prisoners who had been held in the corral. All were exonerated, and the matter was closed.

Columbia. View of the backs of buildings along Main Street taken from near the Fallon House Theater. Disastrous fires swept Columbia in the 1850's, but dozens of historically important brick buildings remain

No mention of Sonora in the early days should pass without mention of Major Richard C. Barry, who was elected Justice of the Peace of Sonora in 1850. There is perhaps no jurist in the country's history gifted with as little comprehension of legal principle as this red-necked Mexican War veteran from Texas.

It is to the man's credit, however, that he could write. For without the little scraps of paper on which he penned his decisions, we would have no record of the strange proceedings of his court.

Columbia. Looking north on Main Street. Legislation to acquire Columbia was passed in 1945 and restoration work on old buildings and streets is still in process. The object of the park project is to turn time back to 1860

Jamestown. Highway 49 skirts the heart of "Jimtown," but the few extra minutes it takes to swing off the highway and drive down the main street are worth it to most Gold Country travelers. Town is known as the "Gateway to the Mother Lode"

The case of Sheriff George Work versus Jesus Ramirez is a classic:

"No. 516. This is a suite for Mule Steeling in which Jesus Ramirez is indited fur steeling one black mare Mule, branded 0 with a 5 in it from sheriff Work.

"George swares the Mule in question is hisn and I believe so to on heering the caze I found Jesus Ramirez guilty of feloaniusly and against the law made and provided and the dignity of the people of Sonora steeling the aforesade mare Mule sentensed him to pay the costs of Coort 10 dolars, and fined him 100 dolars more as a terrour to all evil dooers. Jesus Ramirez not having any munney to pay with I rooled that George Work shuld pay the Costs of Coort, as well as the fine, an in default of payment that the said one mare Mule be sold by the Constable John Luney or other officer of the Coort to meet the expenses of the Costs of Coort, as also the payment of the fine aforesade. R. C. Barry, Justice Peace. John Luney, Constable."

Sonora. St. James Episcopal Church, in use for almost a century, stands at a bend in Washington Street at the north end of town. The graceful structure is said by many to be the most beautiful frame building in the Mother Lode Country

Sonora. This old brick building off Main Street is all that remains of Sonora's Chinatown. It was once a dry goods store where various Chinese articles were sold. (Photo courtesy of Tuolumne County Museum.)

Tuolumne. Here the Sierra Railroad's only passenger car, a converted caboose, waits for travelers. The town, first called Summersville, was the center of a local rush in 1856 and 1857. Today lumber is the town's main interest

What followed is best described by Barry himself in this added note on the case:

"H. P. Barber, the lawyer for George Work in solently told me there were no law fur me to rool so I told him that I didn't care a damn for his book law, that I was the Law myself. He jawed back so I told him to shetup but he wouldn't so I fined him 50 dolars, and comited to goal for 5 days for contempt of Coort in bringing my rooling and dississions into disreputableness and a warning to unrooly citizens not to contredict this Coort."

Jamestown

"Jimtown" as it was and is affectionately known, has a flavor all its own. The meandering main street is lined with old balconied buildings—some of stone and brick dating from the 1850's and many frame structures built in the 1870's and 1880's—that give the town its quaint 19th century character.

The settlement was founded in 1848 by Colonel George James, a lawyer from San Francisco, and like Sonora has remained an active town ever since.

From Jamestown you can travel south through Stent, of which only an old cemetery remains of pioneer days, to Jacksonville; west to Knights Ferry or the Copperopolis road; north to Rawhide; or east to Sonora.

The Stent road is difficult to find without inquiring locally. On this road, still within city limits, you will see Jamestown's old Catholic Church and the Methodist Church built in 1852.

Vallecito and Douglas Flat

If, instead of heading back to Highway 49 when you visit Columbia, you take the road north to Murphys, you'll pass through the old camps of Vallecito and Douglas Flat along the way. The road from Columbia winds down into the raw valley of the Stanislaus River and crosses near the side of Parrots Ferry. The view from the hills on either side of the valley is spectacular.

Jamestown. Rows of balconied frame buildings which line the main street give the town a strong 19th Century flavor. Most of these were built after the Gold Rush died, but one, the Butterfield Building, dates back to 1850

Vallecito, which means "little valley" in Spanish, sits on the banks of Coyote Creek. It was settled in 1850 by Mexican miners, but did not become a prominent camp until a rich strike was made in 1852. Still standing in excellent condition at the south end of town are the Dinkelspiel Store and Wells Fargo Express office. Across the street are the crumbling remains of an old livery stable.

Tuolumne. Large sawmill near Tuolumne is one of many that make up the strength of Gold Country economy. Some will permit visitors to watch the deafening mill operations. Note the logs being pulled up the inclined track from the pond

Vallecito. Dinkelspiel Store and Wells Fargo office buildings are typical of Mother Lode architecture. Look also for the monument built to hold the town's famous bell. This bell was used to call miners to meetings and worship.

Near Vallecito. Spiral staircase with 144 steps penetrates huge limestone cavern at Moaning Caves. Here, as at Mercer Caverns northwest of Murphys, admission is charged. Human skeletons have been found in one of the chambers here

Douglas Flat, a serene little community about two miles from Vallecito, has preserved one stone and adobe building which sits snugly up against the highway. This structure, the Gilleado Building, served as the town store.

Douglas Flat. Gilleado Building was once used as a store. Tale is told that a small opening in the rear of the building was a "shotgun window" provided for an armed guard who watched a gold-laden safe. Across street is the old post office

Murphys

Tall locusts line the streets of this grand old town, and in their shade life goes on much as it has through the decades since the Gold Rush died. In its beautiful setting, Murphys is one of the most charming "live" towns in the Mother Lode.

It was founded by John and Daniel Murphy in 1848, and its rich diggings built the substantial town of brick and limestone buildings that you see today.

The most prominent of the old structures is the famous hotel, now called the Murphys but for many years known as Mitchler's Hotel. It was built by Sperry and Perry in 1855. You can examine the old register and find names of illustrious travelers in the past—Mark Twain, U. S.

Near Vallecito. Here a great diesel lumber freighter has pulled off the road for repairs. You'll meet many if you travel along the roads east of Highway 49 during the week. On some narrower lumber roads, Sunday is the best day to travel

Between Columbia and Vallecito. Bridge crosses the Stanislaus River at the site of Parrots Ferry. The ferry was established in 1860 and operated until 1903. More than one fortune was made in early Gold Rush days by ferrymen

Murphys. Historic marker tells of the Traver Building, oldest stone structure in town. Iron doors and shutters and a sand-covered roof enabled this old-timer to survive the holocausts of 1859, 1874, and 1893

Murphys. The Murphys Hotel has a rich past. It was a favorite stopping place for travelers to the renowned Calaveras Big Trees. It was first called Sperry's and then, for many years, Mitchler's. The hotel's operation has changed little in a century

Murphys. Quiet morning scene looking east along the almost deserted main street. Much of the town's charm stems from the lack of fast-paced commercial activity. Note the locust trees growing at the edge of the street

Grant, Henry Ward Beecher, Thomas Lipton, J. Pierpont Morgan, Horatio Alger, and many others. You might find the entry "Charles Bolton, Silver Mountain,"—a quiet traveler no one would have taken for the notorious highwayman, Black Bart.

Across the street is an old brick and limestone building which was used at the beginning as a bakery and miners' supply store. Farther east is another brick-fronted building with the legend "Stephens Bro's. Cheap Cash Store" painted across the side. This was, at an earlier time, Jones' Apothecary Shop.

The Catholic Church and the Peter Traver Building, both dating back to the 1850's, are among the other notable old buildings.

Murphys, like so many other Mother Lode towns, has a Joaquin Murieta legend. According to one version, it was in Murphys the bandit began his criminal career after he had been flogged for a wrong he had not committed, seen his wife outraged by American miners, and his brother hanged for a robbery he had no part in. Perhaps this didn't really happen to him—no one today can separate fact from fancy in the Murieta tradition—but that sort of lawless cruelty was not unknown. More than one hapless Mexican was forced into a life of crime and revenge because of the ruthlessly brutal treatment handed him by the Americans.

Nine winding and up-and-down miles from Murphys is the town of Sheep Ranch—starting place of the Hearst fortune. It was here that George Hearst, later United States Senator from California and father of the newspaper tycoon, ran the Sheep Ranch Quartz Mine. It is said that this mine was a profit maker from the time the first shovelful was dug.

JACKSON . . first called "Bottileas"

JENNY LIND . . once a grocery store

NEAR CALAVERITAS . . cow country

VOLCANO . . retired hydraulic nozzle

MOKELUMNE HILL . . Mayer

IONE . . "Bedbug" and "Freezeout"

Calaveritas to Plymouth

THE JACKSON AREA

SAN ANDREAS · CALAVERITAS · DOUBLE SPRINGS
JENNY LIND · CAMANCHE · CAMPO SECO · PALOMA
MOKELUMNE HILL · RAILROAD FLAT · WEST POINT
VOLCANO · JACKSON · SUTTER CREEK · AMADOR CITY
IONE · DRYTOWN · PLYMOUTH

San Andreas

San Andreas, one of several Mother Lode towns claiming to be the starting place of the notorious Joaquin Murieta, has little left of the early buildings that give other Gold Country towns their character. The highway is wide and easy to drive in the San Andreas area, but much of the old town was destroyed to make the high-speed stretch.

A huge cement plant south of town employs many San Andreans today. A century ago the rich gravels yielded gold to the Mexican miners who settled the town, then to Americans who crowded them out, and finally to the thousands of Chinese who in the 1860's patiently worked the tailings left by others as valueless.

The old Odd Fellows Hall and the present library-museum-Chamber of Commerce building—a granite and schist structure—stand on the main street as century-old reminders of the town's early importance.

Just west of town, on the hill above Highway 12, is the historic Pioneer Cemetery.

Among the apocryphal stories concerning Joaquin Murieta is one that bears repeating if for no other reason than to point out the proportions the badman's legend has reached.

In San Andreas, it is said, a Frenchman approached Murieta with an offer to supply him with a bulletproof shirt of mail for $1,000 in gold. Murieta accepted, and when the shirt arrived, devised a particularly ingenious way of testing the armor. Forcing the Frenchman to don the shirt, Murieta stood back and fired away with his revolver. The armor worked, however, and when the Frenchman, who had fainted from fright, recovered, he was paid his $1,000 and sent on his way.

As fanciful as *that* tale might be, the conviction of that fabulous highwayman, Black Bart, is a concrete part of San Andreas' history.

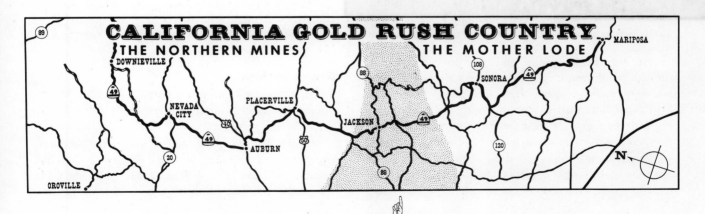

San Andreas. County library, Chamber of Commerce, and museum are housed in the dressed stone building, center. Also on this street are the two-story Odd Fellows building, right, and the adjoining county courthouse

Ironically, his lodgings were just a short distance from police headquarters.

After his release from prison a few years after the the trial, he disappeared. The mild-mannered terror of the highways was never heard of again.

One of the loveliest pastoral areas in the Gold Country lies between San Andreas and the crumbling village of Calaveritas, four miles to the southeast.

Eight miles east of San Andreas on another road is Mountain Ranch, the site of one of the first sawmills to operate in Calaveras County. Today the traveler is constantly reminded that the Gold Country's pay dirt is the soil where tall pines and firs grow.

Double Springs. This stout two-story house was built in 1860 by Alexander Wheat and has housed seven generations of his family. Old county courthouse is located in the rear. Springs that gave settlement its name still flow in front yard

Jenny Lind. These disintegrating adobe walls and the ruins of a tuffaceous sandstone building (pictured on page 46) are about all that is left of Jenny Lind from early days. Note the few remaining patches of crude stucco that still cling to walls

For eight years, 1875 to 1883, the solitary bandit eluded detectives and managed to hold up 27 or 28 stages along mountain roads in the Sierra and the Coast Range.

He was finally caught and sent to San Quentin through the diligence of the sheriff of Calaveras County and a Wells Fargo agent. Bart, who incidentally never fired a shot or harmed a victim, was surprised while opening a strong box in a stage he had stopped near Copperopolis, and in his flight left a handkerchief behind.

By tracing the laundry mark to a San Francisco laundry, they finally caught Charles C. Bolton, who had posed in San Francisco for years as a man with mining interests.

Along the poor road that leads northwest from Mountain Ranch through Jesus Maria to Mokelumne Hill are the sites of the once-thriving camps of Poverty Flat, Whiskey Slide, and Happy Valley.

Double Springs

When Calaveras County was formed in 1850, Double Springs was named county seat, and kept the honor until the following year.

Double Springs lost its official role under interesting circumstances following a contested election between Mokelumne Hill and Jackson to determine which should be named the new seat (Amador County had not yet been formed). With the issue in doubt, a wagon load of determined boys from Jackson arrived in Double Springs to offer the county clerk there a casual libation. One led to another, so the story goes, and it was an easy matter for the Jackson crew to pack up county records and official paraphernalia and hustle it off to Jackson.

Today Double Springs consists of the mellow old two-story stone home built by Alexander Reid Wheat in 1860 that has housed seven generations of his family. Behind the house stands the original court house which was built of camphor wood shipped from China.

The old structure was recently saved from ruin by the Calaveras Grange.

Double Springs lies halfway along a two-mile stretch of road that swings off Highway 12 about five miles west of San Andreas.

Jenny Lind

Jenny Lind, a sleepier village than its bright name suggests, lies 18 miles southwest of San Andreas and about two miles off Highway 8. TV aerials tower over the frame houses with their ancient stone foundations, and nothing but the ruins of the old Rosenberg Building and a crumbling adobe are left of the old town which was the hub of

Campo Seco. This odd little board-and-batten building was Campo Seco's butcher shop decades ago. Across the road are the crumbling remains of several stone buildings, including the two-story Adams Express Company building

Campo Seco. View looking southeast toward the vestiges of the once thriving copper-producing town. Buildings in the foreground are deserted adobes, all that is left of a Chinese quarter. The buildings beyond are still in use

Calaveritas. This old adobe fandango hall is rapidly falling into ruin. Weathering effects of rain on the unprotected walls can be seen. The mud blocks are literally melting away. In a few years, only the foundations will remain

Calaveritas. This is a picture of the same building taken just two years before the one on the left. The view is from the side rather than from the road. In the foreground are remains of similar buildings left unprotected

Calaveritas. Abandoned trestle frames the view as an indifferent cow stalls traffic for a moment. Old-timers here, as in other gold towns, will tell you the area would boom again if only the price of gold were raised from the present $35 per ounce

mining activities on the lower Calaveras.

Though it is named for Barnum's "Swedish Nightingale," the famous singer never came within 2,000 miles of the town.

Campo Seco

Five miles east of Camanche on a rough county road, is another often-bypassed town—Campo Seco. Placer diggings were rich in the early days, but its greatest wealth came from the Penn Copper Mine opened in the 1860's.

In the center of town are several photogenic ruins—one is the remainder of the two-story Adams Express Building that townspeople will tell you was a wide-open speakeasy during Prohibition.

At the southwest end of town are several aged frame residences and California's largest cork oak.

On a small local road northwest of the center of the village are two fairly well-preserved Chinese adobes.

Paloma

Paloma, which was known for years as Fosteria, is today a small collection of undistinguished frame buildings on a wide place in the road, but it began life as a placer mining camp in 1849.

Here, behind the town's historical marker, is a reconstructed arrastra which was once used to crush ore.

The famous Gwin Mine was located on Rich Gulch which leads from Paloma north to the Mokelumne River.

Mokelumne Hill

"Mok" Hill, neither a ghost town nor a booming little metropolis, is one of the most interesting towns in the Gold Country. Its many old stone, brick, and wooden structures and its colorful past give it a special charm.

Many of the buildings in Mokelumne Hill are built of light brown stone known to geologists as rhyolite tuff, a material common to much of the Mother Lode. Best known are the Odd Fellows Hall—first three-story building in the Gold Country; the remains of the Meyer Store; and the famous old Leger Hotel, a stone and brick structure with wooden balconies.

The beautiful wooden Congregational Church, which was built in 1856, sits on columns of fitted stone blocks. Another wooden building of interest is the old French Bakery—one of the most picturesque structures in the town.

In an area that was sometimes ridden by violence and international friction, Mokelumne Hill seemed to have had more than its share. For instance, there was a stretch of 17 weeks, tradition has it, where there was at least one murder every weekend and another time when five people were killed in a week.

The diggings were rich in the "Mok" Hill region, so rich in fact that in certain areas claims were limited to 16 square feet. But this wealth didn't keep the Americans busy with their own work all the time. Unlike many other camps which had one "foreign war," Mokelumne Hill had two.

South of town, the now-vanished camp of Chili Gulch was the scene of the "Chilean War" in which Hillites conquered the stubborn Dr. Concha in 1849. But this was not before several men were killed. Here, at least, there was some justification, because Dr. Concha was working his claim with peon labor and had registered claims in the names of men who were slaving for him. Slavery was one universally forbidden practice in the Gold Country.

The "French War," which occurred two years later, was a different matter.

French miners, who, as a group, had excellent luck in their mining, had raised a French flag above their

"MOK" HILL . . tall Italian cypresses ▶

Between San Andreas and Calaveritas. This four-mile stretch of road passes through one of the most appealing pastoral sections in the Gold Country. Cattle are the main agricultural interest here as in most of the region

Mokelumne Hill. The old French Bakery, left center, is one of the quaintest buildings in the Mother Lodè. The tiny story-book structure is shaded by a heavy growth of trees of heaven. Mokelumne Hill has for decades been a mecca for photographers

Between Mokelumne Hill and Railroad Flat. Small head-frame against the skyline marks one of the Gold Country's many less-important mines. Notice the tailings piled against the hillside. At this altitude lumbering is the main concern

Mokelumne Hill. The I. O. O. F. Hall is the oldest three-story building in the Gold Country and is a splendid example of stone construction. The town was Calaveras County seat from 1854 to 1866 when the honor was given to San Andreas

diggings on a rise, appropriately named French Hill, that overlooks the town. The Americans, using the excuse that the French were defying the American Government, swarmed up the hill and drove the French from their claims. But as far as anyone knows, the excuse was hollow —and only envy and greed provoked the incident.

The Joaquin Murieta tale most often told in Mokelumne Hill is short and certainly more believable than some.

It seems that an improvident miner walked into the now-vanished Zumwalt Saloon, tossed a poke full of gold on a table, and offered to bet $500 that he would kill the bandit Murieta the first time he came face to face with him. With that, an unknown Mexican rose from a card game at a nearby table, grabbed the miner's poke and said, "I'll take the bet." Dashing through the door, he leapt upon his horse and vanished before the crowd knew what had happened. Murieta had won the bet fairly.

Railroad Flat and West Point

If you head east from Mokelumne Hill into the mountains to visit the old settlements of Railroad Flat and West Point, you will pass through an area of scenic beauty and much lumbering activity. Although lumbering is one of the mainstays of Gold Country economy, you can't get a full idea of the scope of the industry until you travel some of the back roads.

West Point, which was named by the famous scout, Kit Carson, has boomed again as a logging center, but buildings which were built with gold taken from rich quartz ledges many decades ago make up much of the town.

Railroad Flat, which was a placer and quartz mining center, is still served by the store and post office that were built in the hamlet's early history.

Railroad Flat. This is the post office of the little settlement which, incidentally, is far from any railroad. Town got its name from a few hundred feet of wooden track laid by a miner to carry ore in a mule-pulled car

Paloma. This reconstructed arrastra once crushed gold-bearing quartz. A horse or mule was hitched to the axle between the wheel and the arrastra's rim. Large boulders attached to the axle ground the ore against arrastra's rock bottom

Volcano

Volcano is unquestionably one of the most important stops in the Gold Country—not only for what it was but for what it is today.

Volcano was rich, as rich as the fabulous "Gem of the Southern Mines," Columbia. More that $90 million was washed from the surrounding country. When the placer workings grew poorer, hydraulic mining tore the soil away from limestone bedrock to be run through sluices.

There are many remains of the early town—stone buildings that line the streets and make Volcano one of the ghostliest of all the ghost towns; the old St. George Hotel (meals and lodging by reservation only); and "Old Abe," the cannon without which the Union might not have won the Civil War.

Volcano's Union volunteers wheeled out "Old Abe" to put down a threatened Confederate uprising. Control of Volcano might have meant that the area's gold would be diverted to the Southern cause. The story is told that in the absence of iron cannon balls, Union men gathered round, river-smoothed stones. "Old Abe" won the battle without firing a shot—his mere presence squelched the uprising.

Volcano claims many "firsts" in California's cultural

West Point. This town was founded in 1845 by Kit Carson at the westernmost point of his expedition that year. Old-timers will point out this building as being over 100 years old. After many sleepy decades, lumbering has reawakened West Point

Volcano. You can't miss the balconied, vine-covered St. George Hotel as you enter Volcano from the south. An old picture, taken before hydraulicking days, shows the hotel in the center of town, but now it's at the southern limits

Almost anywhere in the Gold Country. Here is a striking close-up of the far spread locust with leaves flecked with dew. It was planted in great numbers by American pioneers and is similar in appearance to the Chinese tree of heaven.

development: first public library, first literary and debating society, first astronomical observatory, first "little theater" movement, and more.

Not that Volcano lacked the saloons and fandango halls that filled the miners' idle time in so many of the gold camps. There were dozens of saloons to accommodate the town's thousands of citizens. One of the crumbling stone buildings still standing on the west side of the main street housed two separately operated bars.

Other buildings which line that street are the old jail, an iron structure sandwiched between two-inch board walls; a brewery built in 1856; the Odd Fellows-Masonic Hall, the Adams Express Building (now the Trading Post), and others. All have been marked for your convenience, and the few tradespeople in Volcano are quite willing to fill you in on the town's history.

One of the remarkable things about the Gold Country is the number of people who are intensely interested in preserving what is left of the early days—both the physical remains and the historical tradition. The old-timers who

Volcano. View of the end of Volcano's main street. Building at right was once the Adams Express office. The wooden building, left, is the old jail—built of heavy iron plate sandwiched between inner and outer walls of thick planking

can interminably regale you with Gold Country lore are to be found at every stopping place. But in addition, there are many not-so-old-timers who are encouraging growth of an understanding of the region's significance. Not too many decades ago, there was relatively little interest in the area, but historical societies and similar organizations have grown and the general population has become much more aware of the treasure that remains.

Volcano reflects this awakening and is slowly being restored by private means. But a shadow hangs over the village's future. Any one of three private interests could destroy Volcano as it is today: A power dam below town which would cover it with water, logging activity, and a cement mill have all been seriously considered for the Volcano area.

Volcano's nearest neighbor of any size is Jackson, and during the 1850's the two towns had a sporting rivalry typical of the times. Once a man from Jackson caused quite a stir in Volcano, so reported a Jackson paper at the time, when he produced a $20 gold piece to pay his hotel bill and buy the house a round of drinks. The editor implied that it had been so long since anyone in Volcano had seen a $20 piece that they gathred around the Jacksonian with curiosity and admiration.

Volcano. The ruins of the Wells Fargo office are typical of the limestone skeletons that line the main street and give Volcano its ghostly air. Some reconstruction has been done but most of the buildings have been unused for many years

Martell. Here you see huge logs being dumped from the truck into the mill pond. This mill is one that you can see close-up without traveling far off Highway 49. Conveyor in the background carries waste to the conical burner

It took only a week for the editor in Volcano to straighten Jackson around. It wasn't curiosity or admiration of the gold piece, it seems, it was Volcano's awe that anyone from Jackson should have that much cash in the first place, and further that he would use it to buy someone else a drink and to pay his hotel bill before slipping out of town.

Jackson

If time has made little change in Mokelumne Hill, its feuding neighbor, Jackson, has kept up with "progress" and is a busy trading and entertainment center for the area today. Many of the old buildings along the main streets have new fronts, and bright neon signs compete for the visitor's dollar.

Someone once suggested that life in towns like Jackson, Sonora, Placerville, Auburn, Grass Valley and other business centers more closely resembles life in the Gold Rush days than do the sleepy ghost towns. In these noisy, bustling communities, the crowds that fill the shop-lined streets are more like the lively crowds that thronged through the camps in an earlier day. There is little of the picturesque quality of the old town left on the main streets, but of course there was nothing picturesque about the old town in the eyes of those who lived there a century ago.

Actually, a trip along the side streets in any of these larger communities will reveal the past, and Jackson is no exception.

For many decades two great hard-rock mines, the Kennedy and the Argonaut, were very important in Jackson's economy, but neither has been worked in many years. The huge tailing wheels built at the Kennedy Mine in 1912 (pictured on the back cover) are still standing but haven't turned since 1942. They can be seen from the

Jackson Gate. The 68-foot wheels (see back cover) used to carry tailings from the Kennedy Mine. The wheels, which last turned in 1942, ran at 50 revolutions a minute and were capable of handling 500 tons of solids a day

Jackson. Main street curves through town past old buildings, many of which have new faces. Mining was the main industry in the area, but Jackson's big mines have long been closed. The Kennedy and Argonaut mines were biggest producers

Jackson. St. Sava's Serbian Orthodox Church, first to be built in America, is one of Jackson's most interesting buildings. Another stop that Gold Country travelers should leave time for is the .fascinating Amador County Museum

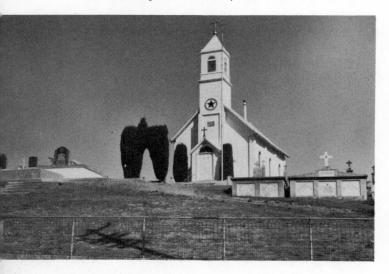

Sutter Creek. This quaint old store, built after Gold Rush days, is only one of many that can be found along the quiet side streets in Sutter Creek. In many larger Gold Country towns, side streets are the most interesting to explore

Jackson Gate road which circles from Jackson to Martell.

Two and a half miles south of Jackson on Highway 49, the Ginocchio Store stands alone as the single remainder of Butte City. A couple of miles farther south is Big Bar on the Mokelumne River. Two old inns are still standing on either side of the bridge at this point. Gardella's is on the southern side and Kelton's on the north. Big Bar was the most important camp on the Mokelumne River.

Although not as old as many of the noteworthy buildings in the Gold Country, St. Sava's Serbian Orthodox Church is well worth visiting when passing through Jackson.

Sutter Creek

Sutter Creek, like Amador City three miles north, is too often bypassed by modern travelers and is actually as charming in its own way as many of the more celebrated Gold Country communities.

The town's name is taken from the man whose name is tied so intimately with the Gold Rush, the pathetic John Sutter.

Sutter mined in the area after he had been unable to maintain his agricultural empire, New Helvetia, which he directed from a fort which has been reconstructed in Sacramento. His hired hands deserted him, and a constant stream of argonauts tramped across his once-productive fields.

He arrived on the creek with a group of Indians to work the placer deposits, but other miners in the area frowned in the practice, viewing it as a form of slavery, and Sutter was forced to leave. As in all his other efforts to salvage something from his once-great empire, he failed.

Another true story with its setting in Sutter Creek is that of Leland Stanford—and success.

Stanford, who had acquired some means as a merchant in Sacramento, financed the Lincoln Mine, but after repeated failures to strike a rich vein, he offered to sell the property for $5,000. His foreman, Robert Downs, had other ideas, however, and he talked Stanford into hanging on for a while longer. The strike was finally made, and on the gold the mine produced, Stanford joined Hopkins, Crocker, and Huntington to build the Central Pacific Railroad and went on to become a U. S. Senator, Governor of California, and to found Stanford University.

JACKSON . . Kennedy Mine close-up

Butte City. What was once a rich gold town is now represented by this single stone structure. Called the Butte Store on the marker, it is also known as the Ginnochio Store. The store, built in 1856, was originally owned by a man named Bruno

Sutter Creek. Main street here is very similar to Jackson's with one exception. Note the relative lack of signs hanging from the shops. Sutter Creek, like neighbors Jackson and Amador City, was an important quartz mining center

Amador City. Interior of one of the Mine House Motel rooms. Motel is housed in the old Keystone Mine Company office building at the south end of town. Proprietor carefully points out that enamelware is for decorative purposes only

Perhaps the most interesting old brick structure is the Hayward Building, the office of Alvinza Hayward, a pioneer in quartz mining who eventually made a vast fortune after suffering many failures.

Amador City

Amador City, straddles Highway 49 halfway between Sutter Creek and Drytown. It was named for Jose Maria Amador, a miner from San Jose, as was the county when the area separated from Calaveras County in 1854.

Neither Amador City nor Sutter Creek was particularly rich in placer deposits, but local quartz supported several rich mines, the most important being the Keystone. A head frame of the mine, which ceased operation almost half a century ago, can be seen on the eastern slope above the south end of Amador City.

The first discovery of gold in the local quartz was made by a minister turned miner who, joined by three other men of the cloth, worked the appropriately named Ministers' Claim Mine.

Ione and Plymouth

Over the Sacramento-Sonora stage route which passed through Jackson, Mokelumne Hill, Angels, and Columbia, more than $265 million in gold bullion is said to have been carried. One of the stops was the Q Ranch, a mile and a half northwest of Ione. The ranch is gone today, but Ione is still prospering.

This little town has been part of the Gold Country since the beginnings, not as a mining camp, but as an agricultural center. It became an important rail center and clay and sand producer.

◀ AMADOR CITY . . 'What's in there?'

Between Lockeford and Ione. This weathered old two-story adobe is perched above one of several roads which fans out from Stockton to the gold fields. Like many Gold Country roads, it's built along an early stage route

Ione. Aged graveyard here is similar to many you can find in the Gold Country. The stories told on the headstones can sometimes give a capsule history of the early community. In some of the cemeteries, dates go back to early 1850's

Like so many other towns that started as temporary camps, Ione's dignified name was chosen only after the townsfolk grew embarrassed about "Freezeout" which had been the successor to "Bedbug." If nothing else, the first two names left little to the imagination as to their inspiration.

The town of Plymouth lacks some of the charm that endears so many others to the traveler, but since the 1850's when it began life as "Pokerville," it has remained the hub of an important agricultural area.

Drytown

Drytown, which lies three miles south of Plymouth, was founded in 1848, and is the oldest town in Amador County.

From its name, you might think it had been settled by men of abstemious habit, but the town actually supported 26 saloons in its prime—a fact suggesting that temperance was not a widespread virtue. It actually took the name from Dry Creek on whose banks the camp was founded.

Plymouth. This building is one of the few relics of the 1850's here. Brick facing and stone side walls were often used in combination, but the brick stepping is unusual. Amador County Fair is held annually in Plymouth in August

There is a fine brick building with floors of marble, looking something like a miniature firehouse, that stands on the east side of the highway in Drytown. It was built in 1851 and was used as a butcher shop for many years. A tiny brick house, very similar to the old butcher shop and still used as a residence, can be found a hundred yards or so on the lane that leads up the hill on the east side of the highway.

Amador City. Now-deserted Imperial Hotel stands at a sharp turn in Highway 49 at the north end of the old town. Another old building, the Amador Hotel, is still doing business. A museum and an old country store also attract tourists

GREENWOOD .. bright Scotch broom

COLOMA . . deserted brick building

GEORGETOWN . old crossroad

VOLCANOVILLE . . short, sad story

STOP

⬆ VIRNER 7
⬅ AUBURN 19
PLACERVILLE 16 ➡

FIDDLETOWN . rammed earth adobe

SHINGLE SPRINGS . . stone shell

Fiddletown to Cool

THE PLACERVILLE AREA

FIDDLETOWN · GRIZZLY FLATS · EL DORADO
DIAMOND SPRINGS · PLACERVILLE · SHINGLE SPRINGS
RESCUE · GOLD HILL · COLOMA · LOTUS · PILOT HILL
COOL · GREENWOOD · GEORGETOWN · VOLCANOVILLE
GARDEN VALLEY · KELSEY

Fiddletown

This sleepy, tree-shaded village lies about six miles east of Plymouth in the center of a prosperous dry farming belt. The hillsides surrounding the town are covered with vineyards and orchards which are tended, in many cases, by descendants of the pioneers who started farming in the 1850's.

Fiddletown's fame must, in part, rest on its name. Founded by Missourians in 1849, it was named by an elder in the group who described the younger men as "always fiddling." It kept the name for almost 30 years, but in 1878 the name was changed to Oleta by the state legislature. This was done at the insistence of Judge Purinton, so the story goes, who had become known in Sacramento and San Francisco, much to his embarrassment, as the "Man from Fiddletown." The old name, whose charm was quickly recognized by Bret Harte and immortalized by him in "An Episode in Fiddletown," was restored in the 1920's.

It was here that a certain Judge Yates reached the limit of his patience in listening to an outlandish whopper and created a classic in courtroom procedure. He heard all he could stand before he finally turned to the witness, banged down his gavel, and said, "I declare court adjourned. This man is a damned liar. Court is in session."

The flavor of the 1850's has been preserved here by several old buildings including a two-story brick store, a one-story brick-faced building with side walls of schist, and an ancient rammed earth "adobe" built by Chinese. The stone buildings are in the center of town on the south side of the main street, and the rammed earth structure is at the east entrance to town. At the other end of the main street is the Schallhorne Blacksmith and Wagon Shop built in 1870.

Fiddletown to Diamond Springs

Beyond Fiddletown about 25 miles and 11 miles to the east of Somerset is Grizzly Flats, now a lumbering town, but

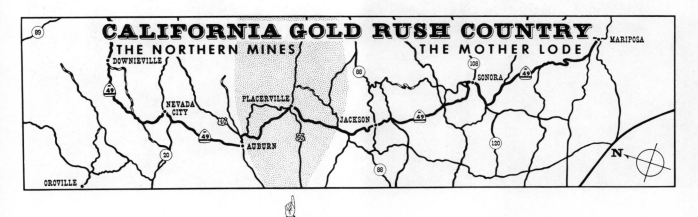

Between Plymouth and Fiddletown. This old frame farmhouse sits across the narrow valley from the little-traveled road to Fiddletown. Ranching and farming commenced early in this section. Note the house's stone cellar and foundation

once a woolly mining camp. Here a few old stone buildings with characteristic iron doors and shutters have weathered the years from the 1850's.

At the Somerset crossing, you can drive west or north toward Diamond Springs and Placerville.

On the road leading north at the site of Pleasant Valley, stands the Norris Hotel built in the 1880's, a favorite stopping place between Placerville and Grizzly Flats.

West of Somerset the road crosses the North Fork of the Consumnes River at Bucks Bar. Below the bridge at this point, you will see unusual granitic formations in the river bed. Natural erosion and chemical disintegration have combined to produce gracefully curved shapes, many of them, like those in the photograph below, resembling contemporary free-form sculptures.

El Dorado

This faded little community, known as Mud Springs when it was the center of rich placer diggings, lies about five miles south of Placerville.

Until 1956, the remains of a block of old buildings

Fiddletown. View looking west through the center of town. Old brick and stone buildings are on the left. Rammed earth adobe—said to have been a Chinese joss house—is on the right. At the other end of main street is an old smithy

Between Somerset and Diamond Springs. Close-up view of a shape formed in the granodiorite bedrock in North Fork of the Consumnes River. Similar erosion can be seen in the bedrock of the Yuba's South Fork east of Highway 49

El Dorado. Interior view of a burned-out shell that stood in El Dorado. Several features of stone construction can be seen here—rough, untrimmed stones in the walls; dressed blocks around the doorways; stucco covering

El Dorado. This was one of a block of burned-out shells that lined the road through El Dorado. Buildings were gutted by fire in 1929 and razed in 1956. Each year sees landmarks of this sort destroyed to make way for modern improvements

stood by the highway, but this landmark was torn down. Other remains of the Gold Rush days, such as the old Occidental Hotel, have disappeared since.

Diamond Springs

Diamond Springs, two miles northeast of El Dorado, has several buildings dating back to the golden 1850's. One of these, the Wells Fargo Express office on the west side of the highway is now an eating place and is camouflaged with a coat of brilliant yellow paint.

The I.O.O.F. Hall, a grand old frame building resting on a foundation of brick and dressed stone, was built in 1852. It has been in continuous use by the Odd Fellows since then.

Placerville

Hangtown, as the county seat of El Dorado County was christened in 1849, was one of the great camps of the Gold Country. It was founded in 1848 by three prospectors, Daylor, Sheldon, and McCoon, who had pushed up from the crowded diggings around Coloma in 1848 and struck it rich—$17,000 in one week.

As soon as the news got about, and news like this never kept for long, the camp was quickly established. It was first called Dry Diggings because here, as in many other areas, the miners had to cart the dry soil down to running water to wash out the gold.

The next year, however, a tough element destroyed the settlement's reputation as a peaceful and law-abiding camp, and the hangings that followed gave the town the name which it hasn't been able to shake in over a century.

No one is quite sure for which hanging the town was named, but tradition brings down the story of several—of the three desperados who robbed a Frenchman named

Cailloux of 50 ounces of dust and were strung up the next morning: of "Irish Dick" Crone, the monte dealer who knifed a man to death over a turn of the cards and then found that his friends didn't have as much influence as he thought they had; and of the two Frenchmen and a Chilean who were hoisted for a crime that no one can remember.

Well, hangings or no, it wasn't long before Hangtown

Placerville. The ivy still growing in front of the Ivy House Hotel on Main Street was planted in the 1860's. Built in 1861, it was first used as a private school, Conklin's Academy. It was transformed into a hotel in the 1890's

Placerville. Although Main Street shows a modern face, most of the buildings were built in the early years. Residential districts are crossed with winding, precipitous streets. Large building on the right is the Odd Fellows Hall

Gold Hill. Located in the midst of fine pear orchard country is this ruined store and the foundation of an old saloon to the right. Road drops down from this point to the Marshall Monument State Park and the town of Coloma

grew to rival San Francisco and Sacramento in population and importance, and in 1854 it became Placerville, a bow to self-conscious pride.

Although most of the old town has been modernized, it is made picturesque by ambling streets that follow old mule trails and wind up precipitous hills. Many of Placerville's historic old buildings are still in use. Next to the P. G. & E. office, the building that now houses a bookstore was built in 1852 and withstood the fire of 1856. From the belfry of St. Patrick's Catholic Church, built

in 1865, still comes the peal of a silver bell donated by early miners. City Hall was built in 1857, and its adjoining structure, now the home of the Judicial Court, was erected in 1862, after Jane Stewart earned the funds for it by driving a herd of horses across the plains.

If you view the buildings which line Main Street from behind—away from the glitter of new facades—you can feel the town's age.

Placerville was the place where three famous men got their starts: Mark Hopkins operated a grocery store here; J. M. Studebaker built wheelbarrows for Hangtown's miners; and Philip Armour ran a butcher shop when the camp was young. All went on to make great fortunes.

Rescue. This tiny crossroads hamlet was named for the nearby Rescue Mine. Surrounded by prosperous farms and ranches, the settlement is little more than a store and post office and this old house which natives say is 100 years old

But two other men in Placerville's history hold higher spots in the hearts of today's Hangtowners.

One was the fabled Hank Monk, the stagecoach driver who scared ten years' life out of the famous editor of the New York Tribune, Horace Greeley, by driving him at breakneck speed along the precipitous drops and hairpin turns on the road from Carson City and answering Greeley's plea that he stop with the order, "Keep your seat, Horace, I'll get you there on time!"

The other was Snowshoe Thompson, whose accomplishments in fact overshadow the fancied deeds of lesser men. For 12 years he tramped across the Sierra with the mail between Genoa, south of Carson City in Nevada, and Placerville during the winter when no one else would or could. He covered the snow-covered 90 miles in three days on the eastward journey and in two days on the return. His generous acts of mercy—he once made the trip from Carson City to Placerville and back for chloroform needed for the amputation of the feet of a man he had just rescued from death—and his endurance and mountain wisdom won't be forgotten. John A. "Snowshoe" Thompson was one of the Gold Country's and California's great pioneers.

Shingle Springs to Coloma

Highway 50, one of the two transcontinental roads that

Near Coloma. The three wine cellars shown here were built at the Vineyard House in 1860, 1866, 1875. The hotel itself burned in 1878 and was rebuilt. The famous hanging of Dr. Crane and Mickey Free took place across the road from hotel

cut across the Gold Country, passes through Shingle Springs, where you'll find the notably preserved two-story Wells Fargo Express building on the south side of the wide highway.

The town was named for the cool spring that flowed near a shingle mill built in 1849. The mill's brick walls still stand.

North of Shingle Springs are the villages of Rescue, Pinch-em-tight, and Gold Hill. Little remains in the first two, but in Gold Hill, which sits in the midst of a very prosperous orchard and cattle-raising area, you will find

Coloma. This monument marks the exact spot on the South Fork of the American River where Sutter's Mill was located. Nearby is the site of the old Wan Lee Store building, now a museum in the James W. Marshall State Park

Coloma. James W. Marshall, who discovered gold here in January of 1848, lived in this cabin until 1868. The building has been restored and is open to the public. A large bronze statue of Marshall is a short distance away

Coloma. View of Emmanuel Episcopal Church looking from St. John's Catholic Church. There are a dozen other old buildings in Coloma and the adjoining Marshall Gold Discovery State Park marked for the convenience of Gold Country visitors

Coloma. Close-up of restored iron doors on the museum in Marshall Gold Discovery State Park. Doors like these were used in pioneer days not only to secure the buildings, but to help check the spread of fires—common occurrences then

the remains of a well-constructed sandstone store built in 1859.

Dropping down toward Coloma on this road, you will pass the entrance to the Vineyard House, an aged hostelry which is again open for guests.

Beyond, a few hundred yards farther down the road, is the entrance to the James W. Marshall State Park, where a huge statue of Marshall looks down on the spot where it all began. Here, the Gold Discovery Museum preserves many relics of the early days. Also at the park are two small stone buildings that once graced the main street of Coloma. Built in the 1850's, both the Wah Hop Store and the Wan Lee Store are now museums.

Coloma

In the fall of 1847, James W. Marshall began construction of a sawmill for John Sutter on the South Fork of the American River. On the 24th of January, 1848, Marshall found gold in the mill's tailrace, and by that simple act, the course of a nation's history was changed.

The secret couldn't be kept, and before summer arrived, the area was filled with '48ers. Before the year was up, the hills for dozens of miles around felt the tread of miners' boots and heard the ring of their picks.

Today Coloma bears little resemblance to the boisterous Gold Rush town of the 1850's. Weathered cottages are half hidden beneath gnarled locust trees in the quiet village where over a century ago, in 1855, one of the Gold Country's most celebrated double hangings was held.

The principals were Mickey Free and Dr. Crane. Mickey Free was a badman—a robber and a murderer the law had finally caught up with in Placerville. Dr. Crane, a teacher, had been convicted of dispatching one of his pupils, a young lady named Susan who had been foolish enough to reject his proposal of marriage.

The town made quite an affair of the proceedings. There was a brass band from Placerville and the crowd was in a holiday mood. But it was the fact that both the

Lotus. Brick store, now unused, built by Adam Lohry in 1859. Nearby tailing piles on the American's South Fork are impressive. Though the road from here to Cool is somewhat narrow and winding, the pastoral scenery is a delight

Pilot Hill. Historical marker stands next to the three-story Bayley House on Highway 49 just north of Pilot Hill. Now a private residence, it was built as a hotel in 1862 by Alcander John Bayley to replace one that burned the year before

doomed came through in the spirit of the occasion that made it a truly memorable event.

With the noose around his neck, Dr. Crane sang several verses of a song he had composed as his departing message and topped off the performance with the shout, "Here I come, Susan!" as the trap fell.

Mickey Free, not to be outdone, rounded out the show with an improvised jig, and then unwittingly climaxed the day by writhing to his death by strangulation after the noose had slipped and failed to snap his neck.

Two small stone buildings on the main street are the best preserved—both were built in the late 1850's and leased to Chinese merchants.

On a side street, you'll see two historic churches: the Emmanuel Episcopal Church—probably the first of this denomination in the Gold Country—and a Catholic church said to be the first of this faith built in the Sierra Nevada region.

El Dorado County has marked all the old buildings of historical interest for the convenience of visitors.

Heading north on Highway 49 from Coloma you will see much evidence of the miners' work—great piles of stones that have been lifted and turned and lifted again in the quest for gold.

The little hamlet of Lotus, south off Highway 49 about half a mile from Coloma, is similar in feeling if not appearance to Jenny Lind—a few old residences still occupied, an old deserted brick store and the falling-down remains of an old two-story stone building known as the Uniontown Hotel. Both towns are off the main trails, both are half forgotten, and both still harbor a couple of souvenirs of greater days.

The road from Lotus to Auburn reveals little except the imposing Bayley House just north of Pilot Hill.

If you turn east at Cool, which is but a wide spot in the highway with a few obscured and forgotten stone foundations and the remains of an old lime kiln, you can circle back to Placerville and see several out-of-the-way gold towns that deserve a visit.

Greenwood and Georgetown

Greenwood was established by an old trapper, John

Between Cool and Greenwood. Here is a pastoral scene you are likely to encounter in this farming country. Stock is diversified, and if you are lucky you may see some sheep. Bartlett pears, in the background, are the heaviest crop

Greenwood, and his two sons who set up store there in 1848. The town grew to respectable proportions in the early years and boasted among other things a well-attended theater. The countryside around is filled with orchards, and Greenwood has carried on since the fevered rush for gold as a tiny and picturesque trading center for the area.

Georgetown, once known by the delightful name of Growlersburg, is a real charmer—not so much for its Gold Rush architecture as for the buildings of the 1860's and 1870's and the beautiful gardens.

However, a brick I. O. O. F. Hall and a few small stores that stand on the north side of the main street date back to the late 1850's.

Opposite the Odd Fellows Hall is the Shannon Knox home, built in 1852—a fine example of the residential style that emerged after the Gold Rush died.

If you drive to Georgetown in spring, you will see the brilliant bloom of Scotch broom which grows in profuse masses in the countryside around the community.

Volcanoville

Seventeen miles east of Georgetown lie the dying remains of Volcanoville. The last half of the drive is quite muddy or dusty, depending on the weather, but you can get a

Volcanoville. Young pine growth surrounds the entrance to this old mine tunnel. The tracks that lead from the opening to the lower left used to carry ore cars from within the mountain. Note the supporting timbers of mine's entrance

Between Volcanoville and Georgetown. Clouds of dust trailing behind cars and trucks is familiar sight on dirt side roads in the Gold Country during summer. In winter, dirt and snow replaces dust, but roads are generally kept in fair condition

Georgetown. You'll find many quaint reminders of the last century in the Gold Country. This tub that you see beyond the doorway in the Georgetown Hotel is a six-footer shipped around the Horn before the Central Pacific Railroad went through

sweeping view of the Sierra landscape from the first eight-mile stretch of road above Georgetown.

Tumbledown shacks, an abandoned post office, and old mine shafts are all that is left of the camp.

The hills all up and down the Gold Country are full of abandoned shafts and tunnels, incidentally, and there is one rule you can apply in regard to all of them if you enjoy your health—*Keep Out!*

Garden Valley and Kelsey

South of Georgetown there are two roads that lead to Kelsey. The poorer and slightly longer road goes through the pretty old town of Garden Valley, which was first known as Johnstown, named for a sailor who founded the early mining camp. When the placers had been worked out, residents turned to truck farming and changed the name appropriately.

Kelsey, or Kelseys Diggings as it was known when thousands thronged to its fields, is another oft-forgotten village with a colorful past. It was here that James Marshall spent his last years in dissolute poverty, and where Miss Margaret A. Kelley, a lifelong friend, assembled a remarkable collection of relics from the Gold Rush days. The collection is now housed at the Gold Discovery Museum at Marshall State Park.

Georgetown. This brick building, dating back to 1859, was originally a hotel known as the Balsar House. The abundance of suitable clays in the area made brick the natural building material here. Building was also used as a theater

Georgetown. Main Street of today's Georgetown leads Northwest to Wentworth Springs, 42 miles away, and beyond to Loon Lake. Known as Growlersburg before 1852, this town was destroyed by fire in 1856, but many buildings date back to late 1850's

Near Georgetown. This leaky flume is reminiscent of the days when hundreds of miles of similar conveyors formed a network over the Gold Country, supplying the mines both power and water. Millions of dollars were spent to build this network

Placerville Area   69

FOREST HILL . . wooden sidewalks

IOWA HILL . . life moves slowly

MICHIGAN BLUFF . . . slumbers now

ALTA . . disintegrating water wagon

AUBURN . . approaching old section

DUTCH FLAT . . grand old trees

Ophir to Dutch Flat

THE AUBURN AREA

AUBURN · OPHIR · FOREST HILL · YANKEE JIMS
MICHIGAN BLUFF · COLFAX · IOWA HILL
GOLD RUN · DUTCH FLAT

Auburn

In the spring of 1848, Claude Chana and a party of Indians traveled northwest from Coloma and were the first to prospect at what today is the city of Auburn. They discovered one of the richest surface deposits in the Gold Country.

During the summer of that year, the gravels at Rich Dry Diggings, as the camp was first named, yielded great wealth to those who took the effort to cart the paydirt to the stream below. It was commonplace for a miner to wash out $1,000 to $1,500 a day. One account tells of four or five cart loads producing $16,000 in a single day.

But the surface placers were quickly exhausted, and it took an accidental discovery to keep the town booming.

A miner named Jenkins had built a ditch and flume to carry water to his claim in Missouri Gulch. A week after he had finished, the water mysteriously ceased to flow. He investigated, and found that the water was pouring into a gopher hole on the flat above the claim. Looking closely, he saw that the bottom of the ditch was covered with coarse gold. In a month, Jenkins took over $40,000 and Auburn's future was fixed.

It wasn't gold that built the modern city you find today, however. From the very earliest days, Auburn's location has made it a natural transporation center. Highway 40, one of the two great transcontinental routes across the Sierra and the Southern Pacific Railroad both pass through Auburn. You can be almost certain, if you stop in town for an hour or so, to hear great engines laboring up the grade pulling a long string of cars loaded for Eastern markets.

Although your first view may be of the modern city built on top of the hill, you won't have any trouble finding the old town which lies below and west of the imposing county court house. There are many old brick and stone structures that were built in the 1850's and 1860's that stand in vivid contrast to the concrete and steel city

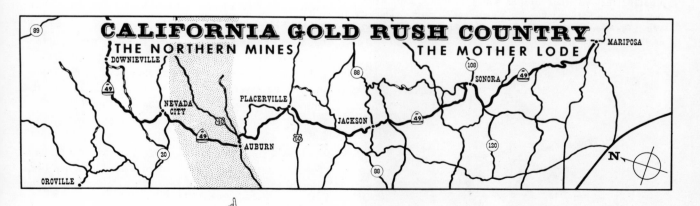

Auburn. This block of buildings on Commercial Street dates back to the 1850's. Building on the corner is the Masonic Hall built in 1853. Next door is the office of the Placer Herald, which has been published continuously since 1852

Ophir. Lonely wall, believed to be the remains of a bakery, is just about all that is left of the early camp first known as Spanish Corral. There is little to indicate that Ophir was the largest settlement in the county in the early 1850's

above. Unlike all the other large towns in the Gold Country, the business center has migrated in Auburn, leaving the early section relatively unmarred and uncovered.

Walk along Lincoln Way and Court Street and Commercial Street. Look for the round-fronted Union Bar built of bricks; the little frame Joss House, distinguished only by the plank with foot-high incised Chinese characters above the door; and the unique, square, four-story fire house.

Make a point of stopping on Highway 49 at the crest of the residential section east of town. The road swings around the hill and at this point you will see the main part of Auburn if you are driving north or first see the sweep of the foothills driving south. Many feel that the panorama from this point can't be matched on any road in all the Gold Country. By just walking a few yards, you can take in a view of the foothills encompassing almost a full 360 degrees.

The Placer County Museum, which is located on the

Auburn. The post office faces on Auburn's old town plaza which shows a strong Spanish influence. View is looking north on Lincoln Way. The tower in the background is the old firehouse pictured on the foldout map

County Fair Grounds in Auburn, has several very interesting exhibits including replicas of rooms from homes built and used in the early mining days and displays of Chinese and Indian objects from the same era.

Although Auburn had a reputation for being a quiet town, as gold towns went, it had its lynchings and badmen like all the rest.

One of the bad actors was Rattlesnake Dick, whose grievances against humanity led him to six years of crime and eventual death from a deputy sheriff's bullet. Inept and misunderstood, Dick was a strange figure. With a dramatic flourish, he dubbed himself "The Pirate of the Placers" at the time of his first holdup, and when found dead six years later he was clutching a note, according to the legend, which read: "Rattlesnake Dick dies but never surrenders, as all true Britons do"—a tragically comic touch to cap his misanthropic career.

Tom Bell was a different species. He was a pioneer, in a sense, because he was the first to hold up a stage coach to rob it of gold. Stages had been coursing through the mountains for years with cargoes of bullion, but not until 1856 was anyone bold enough to try to tap this source of riches.

Tom Bell and five others tried to stop the Camptonville-Marysville stage which was carrying $100,000 in gold, but the unexpected appearance of a strange horseman gave the stage driver a chance to dash through the ambush. There was a furious exchange of gunfire. Several of the passengers were wounded, and one, a woman, was killed.

It took some time for the authorities to catch up with Tom, but they finally did. One of Tom's men had been apprehended and, after a session of "questioning," he revealed Tom's hideout. The daring bandit was quietly captured.

Tom Bell was strung up by the men who nabbed him, but not before he made a full confession of his crimes and had written a letter to his mother. The letter carried a poignant message of repentance and ended, ". . . Give my respects to all my old and youthful friends. Tell them to beware of bad associations, and never to enter into any gambling saloons, for that has been my ruin.

"If my old grandmother is living, remember me to her. With these remarks I bid you farewell forever.

Your only boy,

Tom"

Ophir

Almost due west of Auburn about four miles down Auburn Ravine is Ophir, but you'll have to look hard for the turnoff sign on Highway 40 to find the tiny settlement.

It was once the largest town in Placer County and was for many years an important quartz mining center.

The head frame and building of the Oro Fino Mine and a crumbling stone wall—said to have been a bakery built in the 1850's—are the most interesting things to see there today.

Forest Hill

The road which winds into the hills east of Auburn follows the route of an old turnpike to the lumber town of Forest Hill, beyond which lie two other old mining camps, Yankee Jims and Michigan Bluff. The trip up the Forest Hill divide is through thick pine forests and the view of mountains and canyons is spectacular, but the area is often overlooked by travelers through the Gold Country.

Forest Hill was a prosperous mining and trading center which boomed in 1853 after winter storms and resulting landslides exposed free gold at the head of Jenny Lind Canyon. Since then more than $10,000,000 has been taken from the gravels within a radius of about two miles.

A large bell, once considered as clear and as beautifully toned as any in the Gold Country, sits on the ground near the site of the Forest Hill Church which burned recently. It is said that when the air was right, the bell, which hung in the church's belfrey, could be heard for twenty miles.

Yankee Jims

Yankee Jims, which is just three miles from Forest Hill along the road to Highway 40, sprang into being under strange circumstances, but the story is a credible one.

Near Auburn. The Foresthill road, lower right, turns off Highway 49 just past the American River bridge three miles northeast of Auburn. The bridge downstream from the Highway 49 bridge is an abandoned railroad crossing

Forest Hill. According to a historical marker "the bell in this old church" was cast in Russia in 1860. The church is gone, victim of a recent fire, and the inscription on the bell in English reveals that it was cast in Troy, New York.

Yankee Jims. This tiny collection of old structures sitting on the ridge between the American River's North and Middle Forks is all that is left of one of Placer County's largest gold camps. The state's first mining ditch was built here

Michigan City. This picture, taken from an 1854 daguerreotype, shows an early, small-scale hydraulic operation. Gold-bearing gravel is washed from "The Bluff" with a powerful stream of water carried to the scene by flume, upper left

Yankee Jim, who was not, in fact, a Yankee but an Australian, was a low character. Rather than dig and wash the good soil of the American River, he stole horses, and nothing was lower than a horse thief in those days. Horse thieves, if caught, were summarily strung up.

Yankee Jim was an old professional, and if one of his victims hadn't bothered to make a careful investigation, Yankee Jim might have gone on indefinitely. But the victim found his horse, and others, too, in a corral hidden away in a high and remote part of a ridge. Yankee Jim hightailed it out of the country just in time to save his neck, and in a way it was sort of a shame.

Because it wasn't much later that a miner wandered into the old corral to do a bit of prospecting and found the ground was rich in free gold.

A crowded camp mushroomed up and a fortune was taken from the diggings—a fortune that could have been Jim's, if it had occurred to him to try his hand at a little honest labor.

Michigan Bluff

The tumbledown remains of Michigan Bluff are at the end of a seven-mile road east of Forest Hill. Best remembered for the extensive hydraulic mining which tore away at the mountainsides in the area, the town consists today of a few frame buildings left from the 1880's when the Monitors were muzzled.

Between 1853 and 1858, approximately $100,000 in bullion was shipped from the region each month.

Michigan City, which was the original town site half a mile away, had its foundations undermined by furious hydraulicking during those five years, so in 1859 the population moved *en masse* to a location higher on the brow of the hill. They called the new camp Michigan Bluff.

You'll see the carefully labeled Stanford Store and residence, but some historians believe that this is merely a wishful identification with Leland Stanford. He actually did own a store and house in Michigan City from 1853 to 1855, but these buildings could hardly have survived to this day.

Colfax. This is the town that sprang up when the railroad failed to pass through nearby Illinoistown, which until 1865 was the area's important transportation center. Colfax was known as Camp Twenty while the railroad was being built

Between Iowa Hill and Colfax. The nine-mile road from Highway 40 to Iowa Hill crosses the North Fork of the American River on this one-way suspension bridge. It's hard to believe the sleepy site of Iowa Hill was once a boom town

Colfax

About 16 miles northeast of Auburn on Highway 40 is Colfax, an important agricultural and lumber shipping center.

The town, which was named for Schuyler Colfax, Vice President under U. S. Grant, is near the early settlements of Alder Grove and Illinoistown, and grew into its role as a shipping center in the 1860's after completion of the Central Pacific Railroad.

Illinoistown was a wagon train terminus, and goods were transferred there to mules to be carried farther into the hills. Many of these winding mule trails were made into toll roads, one of which is the present county road that leads east to Iowa Hill.

Iowa Hill

Iowa Hill was one of the late camps to be established in the Gold Country. Gold was not discovered there until 1853, but the ridge on which the town sits was rich, and many camps flourished nearby through the 1850's and 1860's.

Fires have been part of Iowa Hill's history since 1857, when a huge conflagration burned the town to ashes. Only one old brick building on the main street is left to remind the few dozen citizens and the occasional traveler of the golden past. The last fire was in 1922, but a few residences were spared.

More than $20,000,000 in gold was taken from the ridge, mostly by hydraulic mining. An estimated $30,000,000 still remains, but it will probably remain locked in the gravel until the anti-debris laws are repealed.

On Banjo Hill above the few quaint white frame houses that make up the hamlet is the pioneer cemetery which, as in many other old camps, provides the most stirring touch with the past.

Gold Run

The rich deposits of gold-bearing gravel along an ancient stream bed near Gold Run made the town boom right up to the court-imposed end of hydraulic mining in 1884.

Raw cuts made by the hydraulickers have been softened by the weather and coniferous growth, but the old diggings are still an awesome sight.

Above the man-made canyons on Highway 40 sits the village that produced over $15,000,000. But only the little shingled Union Church, built by miners' contributions, is left as a memento of early days.

Dutch Flat

Dutch Flat, one of the most lovable old towns in the Northern Mines is just a mile off the much-traveled Highway 40 about 30 miles above Auburn.

The town takes its name from the German miner, Joseph Dorenbach, and his countrymen who commenced washing the placer deposits there in 1851. Like many Gold Country "Flats," it's anything but a flat town.

Dutch Flat was an important stage stop on both the Donner Pass and Henness Pass routes until the railroad pushed on to Cisco farther up in the mountains. But hydraulicking continued into the 1880's and kept the town alive and bustling.

All of the buildings along the main street have spanned the century—or almost. There are older, more colorful, quainter structures up and down the Sierra foot-

Dutch Flat. Barren bank left by hydraulic miners north of town is reflected in the waters of a man-made lake. Services are held here on Easter Sunday. It has been estimated that $30 million remains in the ancient river bed

Iowa Hill. Like other rich hydraulic centers, Iowa Hill had continuous need for a strong vault. Note the old padlock on the vault's door next to the boy's head. Marker was placed by the Placer Centennial Commission in 1948

hills, but at very few places in the Gold Country will you see such a block of well-preserved buildings, dating from the 1850's, as you'll find in Dutch Flat.

Dutch Flat is the only major Gold Country camp that never suffered a serious fire, even though miners called it "Tinder City" in the early days when all buildings were built of wood.

Along this street are the old Dutch Flat Hotel, the Nichols Bank, and I.O.O.F. Hall. The large restored mansion that stands up the street was built by one of the Towle brothers, lumber barons of a later day.

Only a few crumbling ruins mark the site of Dutch Flat's Chinese quarter which sheltered 1,000 souls while the railroad was being built. The bones of Chinese who died in this foreign land have long since been dug from the pine-shrouded Chinese cemetery adjoining the American cemetery above town and carried back to China for burial.

Dutch Flat. This well-preserved town was one of the largest in Placer County in the middle 1860's. It was an important staging center in addition to being one of the richest hydraulic mining centers. Millions were taken from surrounding hills

Dutch Flat. Main Street of Dutch Flat. On left is the Dutch Flat Hotel, built in 1852 by Charles Steffens. At the height of its prosperity, the town supported two hotels and dozens of other businesses of all descriptions

Dutch Flat. Like most Gold Country towns, Dutch Flat was proud of her cultural and social attainments. It had its I.O.O.F. Hall, shown here, three schools, three churches, and an opera house. It also kept two breweries and 17 saloons busy

"HUMBUG" . . quiet since 1884

ROUGH AND READY . . . landmark

NEVADA CITY . . quaint 'Red Castle'

ENGLEBRIGHT DAM . . on the Yuba

YUBA RIVER . . South Fork runs clear

WASHINGTON . tailings near bridge

Timbuctoo to Graniteville

THE NEVADA CITY AREA

GRASS VALLEY · ROUGH AND READY · FRENCH CORRAL
BRIDGEPORT · SMARTVILLE · TIMBUCTOO · BROWNS VALLEY
STANFIELD HILL · OREGON HOUSE · DOBBINS
CAMPTONVILLE · NORTH SAN JUAN · NEVADA CITY
WASHINGTON · NORTH BLOOMFIELD
GRANITEVILLE · NORTH COLUMBIA

Grass Valley

The accidental discovery of gold-bearing quartz in 1850 on a hill in Grass Valley is one the Gold Country's often-repeated stories. The discovery itself was a simple matter; but because of it, Grass Valley has been a great and consistent gold producer ever since.

In 1850, the settlement was a tiny mining camp whose lush grazing pastures had attracted the first party of prospectors who passed through in 1849. The surface diggings were not rich, however, and it remained for a man named Knight to stub his toe one night, while in pursuit of a wandering cow, to inadvertently make the find that led to Grass Valley's boom. After he stumbled, the glitter of shining metal in the piece of quartz he had broken loose took his mind off the cow. Back in his cabin, he crushed the stone and washed gold from the fragments to confirm his guess.

The news spread quickly, and from that time on quartz mining became the camp's sole interest. It built

what today is the biggest city in the Gold Country.

Modern faces have covered many of the old brick buildings which went up after the disastrous fire of 1855, and as a result, there is little that is quaint or charming about the town. Perhaps no other Gold Country city has kept abreast of modern changes so persistently as has Grass Valley.

The fire that wiped out 300-odd frame buildings that made up the early community has been called the most disastrous of all the many that ravaged the Gold Country camps during the Rush.

But even with changes, narrow meandering streets and a few old structures will remind you of the town's age.

One two-story frame house which has been saved was the residence of Lola Montez. The house, which is at the corner of Walsh and Mill streets, was a one-story structure when she lived there, but unlike the "Bret Harte Cabin" in Second Garrote or the "Leland Stanford Store"

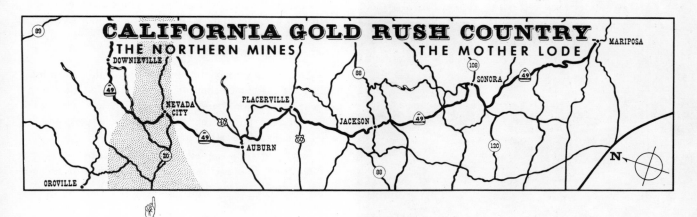

79

Rough and Ready. Tumbledown old frame building lists to port in the shadow of a huge poplar tree, known to all as the "Slave Girl" tree. Many stories are told about the tree, but all must be considered part of the romantic Gold Country lore

Grass Valley. The discovery of gold-bearing quartz in 1852 set Grass Valley's future for the next century. Today most mines, like the North Star Mine shown here, are either closed or are working on a limited basis

Grass Valley. Here at the famous Idaho Maryland Mine, you see inclined elevators which drop far into the earth. Other quartz mines that operate or operated in the Grass Valley area: Empire, Old and New Brunswicks, Bullion, Spring Hill

in Michigan Bluff, the "Lola Montez House" claim has been verified.

Lola Montez—born Eliza Gilbert in Ireland—was a creature of remarkable beauty, and her past and subsequent behavior made her the talk of the camps after her arrival in San Francisco in 1853.

Before coming to America, Lola had been the mistress of Ludwig of Bavaria for two years and later presided over soireés where the continent's foremost artistic and literary figures held sway—Franz Liszt, George Sand, Victor Hugo, and Alexander Dumas were among her intimates.

Her success in San Francisco with the much-heralded Spider Dance had not been the smash she had expected. In fact, her talents were burlesqued by others on the city's stages. After receiving a mixed reception in Sacramento and Marysville, she descended on Grass Valley and, forsaking the theater, spent two years in "retirement" there.

Of course, the people of Grass Valley were very conscious of the personality that had settled in their bower, and it was with both awed admiration and fear that she was greeted. The story that her welcome was established after she had danced the tarantella at the door of an objecting minister seems farfetched, but it cannot be denied that the story fits the Montez legend.

She may never have horsewhipped an editor for printing some inaccuracy about her, but stories like that have a way of persisting, and few doubt its truth. Certainly she did keep grizzly cubs and monkeys as pets, and it is a fact that she was a bigamist.

But apart from the less important parts of this biography, there is one chapter which must remain to her eternal credit. Two doors from Lola's house lived a family named Crabtree: John and Mary Ann and their little daughter, Lotta.

Lotta was a merry child, and it wasn't long after Lola bought her house that she discovered the talent of this bubbling, irrepressible little girl. Lola taught her bits of dances and songs and often let her perform for her celebrated guests. Legend has it that she took the tot to Rough and Ready where she danced for the miners on a blacksmith's anvil. Mary Ann Crabtree trusted Lola and believed her when she predicted great success as an actress for the black-eyed darling.

About a year later, John Crabtree, an ineffective dreamer who was more of a burden than a help to his family, decided to move to Rabbit Creek, now known as La Porte. This might have seemed like disaster to Mary Ann, who had great hopes for her little girl, but it led to a triumph—the first in a long lifetime of triumphs for Lotta Crabtree. It was in Rabbit Creek that she captured the miners' love.

The rough men of the camp showered the stage with coins and nuggets after she had finished her first performance there, and her reputation was made.

Lotta went on from her successes in the mines and in San Francisco to New York and international fame. From the rude beginning on a rough board stage, dancing and singing and laughing by candlelight, Lotta built a fortune of $4,000,000. She died in 1924, a gracious old lady of 79 years.

But for Lola Montez, who first recognized and encouraged and trained the child, fate was not kind.

Bridgeport. This old shingled bridge is claimed to be the longest single-span covered bridge in California. This road follows the old Marysville-Nevada City stage route through French Corral. Note the sense of strength the graceful arch imparts

She left Grass Valley for Australia in 1855, apparently tired of retirement. But she failed there and failed later as a lecturer back in the United States. Then her health began to deteriorate, and in 1860 the fabulous Lola, whose

Near Smartville. Englebright Dam backs up the Yuba into a lake almost ten miles long. There are no improvements of any kind in the area, but it's a popular place with outboard motor enthusiasts. Dam originally built to settle debris

name will always be remembered in the Gold Rush tradition, died penniless in New York.

Grass Valley wasn't all gold miners and actresses, though, for it can claim Josiah Royce. Although many Gold Country towns boast of men who became merchants and financiers of tremendous wealth, only Grass Valley produced a scholar and thinker of the stature of this great American philosopher who was born here in 1855, a son of pioneers.

Rough and Ready

The Free State of Rough and Ready, whose impetuous declaration of independence from the Union in 1850 was mentioned at the beginning of the introduction to this book, is nestled in a dip in Highway 20 amidst some of the loveliest rural countryside in the Gold Country.

The quiet little village, which appears as anything but what its name implies, was founded by a band of Mexican War veterans who took the name from their ex-commander, General Zachary Taylor—"Old Rough and Ready."

It was here that little Lotta Crabtree is said to have danced and sung on a blacksmith's anvil and captivated the miners who had gathered about.

Along a Gold Country River. This is a modern version of the "Long Tom" sluice box that was used to wash pay dirt during the Gold Rush. There are still hundreds who spend all or part of the year working Gold Country streams for "color"

Timbuctoo. This is how a lithographer saw Timbuctoo in 1867. The four-in-hand Concord stage is passing the Wells Fargo office in the Stewart Brothers Store building. This is the only building you will find standing today

Timbuctoo. The town shown in the old lithograph above consists today of this one old building—the Stewart Brothers Store. It has been partially restored to check deterioration. Painted sign, center, reads, "GOLD DUST BOUGHT"

On the south side of the highway, there is an old locust tree marked: "The Slave Girl Tree." According to a salty tale told by Rough and Ready old-timers, the tree grew from a switch thrust into the ground by a girl named Caroline who was the daughter of a plantation slave brought to the diggings by his master. According to the tale, which from this point on has no connection with the tree, Caroline eventually migrated to San Francisco where she became blind, accidentally caught her dress on fire, and drowned in the well into which she had leaped to put out the fire.

Well, it could have happened.

French Corral

French Corral, which is ten miles north on a road that leaves Highway 20 about three miles west of Rough and Ready, was named, appropriately enough, for a Frenchman who built a corral for his mules there in 1849.

The Milton Mining and Water Company office building, later used as a store, was once the terminus of the first long-distance telephone line in California.

The Wells Fargo building and the school, which was originally a hotel, both date back to the 1850's.

Southwest of French Corral about two miles is an old covered bridge at the site of the old camp of Bridgeport.

Smartville and Timbuctoo

Ten miles below Rough and Ready, off Highway 20 about half a mile, is Smartville, a little hillside community of frame buildings that once served 1,500 miners. The stately white Church of the Immaculate Conception, which overlooks the main road through town, was built on the stone foundations of the original church built in 1861.

Hydraulic mining commenced in the 1860's and the town thrived until 1883. There were some 16 saloons, a theater, dance halls and general stores, but today only a store and post office remain.

To reach Timbuctoo you have to return to Highway 20 and drive half a mile farther west, then turn right at the historical landmark sign. The Wells Fargo office, which is all that is left of the once-prospering stage stop, has been partially restored. It is said that the town was named after an African miner who was the first to pan for gold there.

Browns Valley to Camptonville

The road between Browns Valley and Camptonville is part of the old stage route between Marysville and Downieville, and although there are only a few tattered remains of the once-great string of stage stops, the 35-mile drive is an adventure.

At the Browns Valley end, the country is gently rolling farm and ranch land, but at the summits above either side of Bullards Bar Dam, you are high in the pine forests of the lower Sierra.

The road is a natural one, following the turns and dips of the terrain. At the higher altitudes, except when an occasional lumber freighter comes roaring along, you can imagine with little difficulty what it must have been like to lurch around the sharp turns in a Concord coach. When you look into the valley of the North Fork of the Yuba

Near Bullards Bar. This stretch of shaded road is on the ridge east of Bullards Bar Dam. The huge dam replaced the last of several toll bridges located near the bar which was one of the most famous on the North Fork of the Yuba

North San Juan. This ruin, which is viewed from the rear, is right on Highway 49. It was originally a store, later converted into a garage. When San Juan boomed, a band gave evening concerts from the balcony on the front of the building

Nevada City. The smaller of the two old buildings is the Ott Assay office which operated for a century in the same spot. It was here that the fabulously rich Comstock Lode silver ore was first analyzed in 1859

Nevada City. View from the road entering town from the south. The church, upper center, is St. Canice Catholic Church built in 1864 after fire razed the original edifice. Union Hotel, lower right, occupies a site where boarding house was built in 1850

you'll be glad you have a low gear and good brakes and don't have to trust six horses and an unknown driver for safe descent.

Stanfield Hill and Oregon House are two of the old stops that can still be located easily.

At Stanfield Hill, an old stone foundation on one side of the road and a lushly overgrown farmhouse on the other mark the site. At Oregon House, a little post office and residence stands on the site of the popular hostelry that gave the stop its name.

Dobbins, which is the last stop before the winding road climbs into the forested mountains, is a comparatively busy place with a number of homes and several places of business.

Nevada City. The Nevada County Historical Museum is housed in the Number 1 Firehouse on Main Street. The Number 2 Firehouse, built in 1861, is on Broad Street. On display are tools, clothing, records, and other relics from pioneer days

Nevada City. The modern County Court House stands in severe contrast to most of Nevada City's buildings which are representative of a century-old architectural style. The town has been county seat since the county was formed in 1851

Washington. A wooden frame and galvanized iron roof protect this old stone building on Washington's main street. The town, built on the banks of the South Fork of the Yuba River, was founded in 1849. Today it's a lumbering center

The forest through which you travel at the top of grades on either side of Bullards Bar Dam is typical of the Sierra at that altitude. Manzanita, some of it dead and bleached white by the weather, and pines are everywhere, and the floor is covered with patches of squaw's carpet and mountain misery, whose odor you won't forget.

Camptonville

Camptonville, which is across Highway 49 from the rest of the road, is a town that twice survived the attack of hydraulic Monitors by moving each time before the foundations were washed away.

You'll find two monuments side by side on the west end of town. One is erected to the memory of Lester Pelton, inventor of the Pelton wheel which was so important in the development of hydroelectric power equipment.

The other was dedicated by E Clampus Vitus (of which more will be said) to William "Bull" Meek—as the marker reads, "Stage Driver—Wells Fargo Agent—Teamster—Merchant."

He is believed to be the only regular stage driver in all the area never to have been robbed by holdup men. Some old-timers will tell you that he escaped being robbed because he regularly carried supplies to a Downieville bordello. According to this theory, the madam and her ladies are supposed to have used their influence on the region's badmen to keep their contact with the rest of the world safe.

North San Juan

Despite its Spanish name, North San Juan was as Yankee a town as any in the Northern Diggings. It was named San Juan, it is believed, by a veteran of the Mexican War who saw a resemblance to a hill in Mexico on which a

Washington. Here past and present are significantly juxtaposed. The modern lumber mill's burner is built over a great mound of boulders left behind by patient Chinese who were the last to work over Washington's diggings

Relief Hill. These old frame buildings are just about all that is left in the Relief Hill area. It is believed that a second relief party sent out to aid the Donner party survivors met the refugees and their rescuers here

prison of that name stood. "North" was tacked on when the town acquired a post office in 1857.

When San Juan Ridge's hydraulic diggings were being worked, the town was a center for thousands, and it is still the trading center for the few hundreds who still remain in the area.

The old town hall, along with the Wells Fargo building and what was once the Masonic Hall, stands on the north side of the highway and is considered one of the finest examples of early brick architecture in the Gold Country.

Nevada City

Five miles north of Grass Valley, Nevada City sits perched on the banks of Deer Creek. The highway between the towns was once the most heavily traveled section of road in the state, and although some of this stretch is lined with modern buildings of all descriptions, it's not too hard to picture the mule-drawn wagons and the men on foot and horseback trudging on to Deer Creek Dry Diggings as Nevada-City was first known.

Your first glimpse of Nevada City from the south is as picturesque a view as you will see in the Gold Country. Very few will disagree that Nevada City is the most charming of all the major Gold Rush cities, and in all likelihood your first impression will confirm this.

The town is elderly in feeling, and its old age is

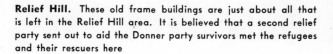

Diggings on San Juan Ridge. Once these diggings were considered an ugly blot on the landscape, but time has weathered and softened the great scars cut into the hills by unrelenting hydraulic Monitors. Diggings, lower left, are near North Columbia. The other three pictures are the Malakoff Diggings which can be seen from the road west of North Bloomfield

gracious and dignified. The residential sections are made up of wonderful many-gabled, two or more story frame houses that have been maintained over the decades, and the downtown is the least altered of all the larger camps that have survived as modern communities.

The steep, meandering streets of the business section are still busy, but the old brick and stone structures which date back to the 1850's have changed little.

The area was first prospected by James W. Marshall in 1848, but he failed to discover the wealth that within two years attracted thousands of miners to work the placers.

In 1850, the miners renamed the camp Nevada, which it remained until ten years later when the newly formed state to the east took the same name. With great reluctance and not without a fight, the town of Nevada gave in and added "City" to its name. Don't make the mistake of asking one of the citizens if the town was named after the state. The subject still rankles.

There are numerous buildings with a rich history within a radius of a few hundred yards, the most famous of which are: the Ott Assay Office, where ore from the Comstock Lode was first analyzed and found rich in silver; the National Hotel, with its balconies and balustrades reaching out over the high sidewalks, still one of the best hotels in the Gold Country after a century of service; the old fire houses, one of which is now a museum with a remarkable collection of historical remnants of Gold Rush days and is an excellent information center.

One of the most colorful characters in early Nevada City (or for that matter, Gold Country) history was Madame Eleanore Dumont, the lady gambler. She arrived in Nevada City one day in 1854, young, well-dressed,

North Bloomfield. Shingles are falling away from the roof of this old house. The town, originally called Humbug by disappointed miners, was big and prosperous until 1883, when the courts halted all hydraulic mining in the state

Graniteville. At an elevation of almost 5,000 feet, Graniteville is one of the highest gold towns in the region. Snow lies on the ground well into spring (this picture was taken in May) and during the winter blocks the roads leading to the little settlement

and of polite demeanor. But it wasn't long before the town learned of her purpose. She opened a *vignt-et-un* parlor that became the talk of the mines. Charming, proper in every way except that she was a professional gambler, Madame Dumont was a truly unique figure.

For two years she dealt the game, known also as "twenty-one" or "blackjack," to willing Nevada City miners, but as the surface deposits began to peter out, business slowed, and in 1856 Eleanore Dumont, who was to be remembered by all as Madame Moustache, moved on.

The name, which followed her in later years as she traveled from camp to camp, was prompted by the dark, downy line on her upper lip, and it summed up the lack of respect that grew as the years tarnished the once-bright young woman.

No one is quite sure where she went. Tradition has it that she traveled all over the West from one boom town to the next, always gambling, always dealing the same game.

Twenty-five years after she first stepped off the stage

Between North Bloomfield and Washington. Blooming dogwood brightens this densely wooded section near North Bloomfield in spring. Farther on toward Washington, the road is cut into a sparsely wooded rocky bluff above the Yuba River

in Nevada City she was found dead near Bodie, a suicide.

No one knows where she came from, few lamented her death. But the chapter she wrote in Gold Country history, which started with brilliance and ended in drab and tragic obscurity, is a permanent part of the book.

Washington

Thirteen miles east of Nevada City, a winding road leads from Highway 20 on Harmony Ridge down to Washington on the banks of the South Fork of the Yuba.

Just before the turnoff, there is a stopping place on the north side of the road where you can pause and take in a magnificent view. If you look northeast from this spot, you can see across all three forks of the Yuba and the mountains between to the jagged Sierra Buttes, 20 air miles away.

Washington is a lumber town today, but all around are the miniature mountains of boulders that miners a century ago piled up in their back-breaking search for gold.

In Washington there are two old stone buildings— one with the date 1867 carved into its keystone—which were once saloons but today are deserted. An old wooden church which dates back to early mining days stands above the road at the north end of town, but like the saloons it is slowly falling into decay.

A twisting dirt road leads up a precipitous cliff west of Washington to Relief Hill and North Bloomfield and is typical of the one-lane roads you will find in the section. Dusty in the summer, sometimes impassably muddy in the winter, the road is not for the meek. If you want to travel on this road or one like it, do it on a Sunday when the great diesel lumber trucks are not working. It is quite an experience to meet one of these giants as you come

around a turn that looks straight down a rocky cliff to the river 500 feet below.

North Bloomfield

There are several ways to get to North Bloomfield from the west, and regardless of the route you choose, you will travel on a well-graded dirt road through forest lands that once echoed with the roar of great hydraulic Monitors but today are ghostly silent.

The road from Nevada City follows an old stage route, but unless you return by the roads that lead to North San Juan, you will miss what remains of Tyler, known as Cherokee in the 1850's, and North Columbia. In each of these old camps, only a few anonymous frame buildings and abandoned hydraulic mining equipment are left.

Even though North Bloomfield is still inhabited and is in some ways one of the pleasantest communities in the Gold Country, there is a kind of lonely, other-world feeling that many visitors sense when they arrive there. Perhaps it is the silence and complete lack of commercial activity. Or perhaps it is that you have just passed, and probably viewed in awe, the astonishing Malakoff Diggings, where multi-colored, many-spired cliffs rise 600 feet above milky blue lakes—all the creation of man.

Some find it inconceivable that men could have carved the mountains so, but the power of water driven under great pressure which played against the mountainsides ate away the gravel in fantastic bites. Some of the nozzles were nine inches in diameter and delivered over 30,000 gallons of water a minute. On this scale even gravel that would yield only ten cents a cubic yard could pay the operators a substantial profit.

But the debris which choked the waterways and ruined farms in the Sacramento Valley below finally brought about the halt to hydraulic mining in 1884. Today large trees soften the devastation and desolation of this man-made wonder.

Beyond North Bloomfield a road leads east to Relief Hill and Washington and another climbs northeast to the remote hamlet of Graniteville.

Beyond Graniteville. Fording creek, a pleasant change of pace on country road that leads to Bowman Lake and campground on Jackson Creek. Beyond, the route is for drivers who know mountain roads, and for sportsmen seeking less heavily fished waters

Bowman Dam. The new concrete dam rises far above the cribbing of the original structure built by miners in the 1860's. Flume in foreground, built in 1926, carries water from Bowman Lake to Lake Spaulding, 20 miles south

DOWNIEVILLE . . quiet summer day

GOODYEARS BAR . near Highway 49

JOHNSVILLE . . unusual graveyard

SIERRA CITY . . two-story landmark

FOREST . . almost hidden by trees

Alleghany to Johnsville

THE DOWNIEVILLE AREA

GOODYEARS BAR · FOREST · ALLEGHANY · DOWNIEVILLE
SIERRA CITY · JOHNSVILLE

Goodyears Bar to Alleghany

The easiest way to reach the old high-country camps of Goodyears Bar, Forest, and Alleghany, is to turn south off Highway 49 on the Goodyears Bar road three miles west of Downieville.

You'll cross the Yuba's North Fork at Goodyears Bar, which was named for the brothers who settled there in 1849. The camp boomed when the news got around that $2,000 was taken from a single wheelbarrow load. But the surface diggings gave out here as they did all over the Gold Country, and you will find only a few frame buildings and the handful of people who still live here.

Forest, a lively camp in the 1850's, is about ten miles across the ridge above Goodyears Bar. The town flourished only until a bigger strike was made on the south side of Pliocene Ridge. Within a few years of the new discovery, Forest's population had moved to Alleghany.

Only a dozen or so people live there today, and many of the old buildings are locked. But you can peer through the windows of some, including the old lodge hall, a tobacco and confectionery shop, a school, and a weathered church.

Five miles beyond is Alleghany, an active gold mining town. The 16-to-1 Mine here has been producing since 1896.

Alleghany is built on the bias. The houses balance precariously on side hill terraces, and threaten to fall into the ravine at any minute. The streets are narrow and wind down from one level to the next. Below the town at the bottom of the ravine is Kanaka Creek, named for a group of Hawaiian prospectors who mined the creek bottom in 1850.

There are two routes you can take out of Alleghany if you don't wish to return to Highway 49 via Goodyears Bar.

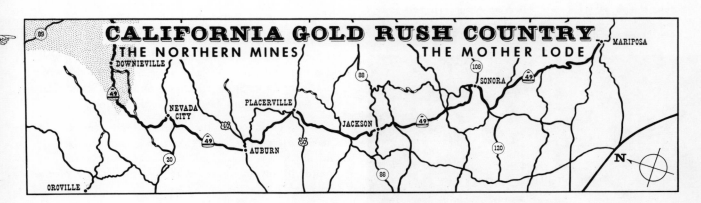

Forest. Established in 1852, Forest flourished until rich diggings were found on the other side of Pliocene Ridge at the site of present-day town of Alleghany. Forest's population migrated over the ridge to found the other town

Between Alleghany and North Columbia. Foote's Crossing Road parallels, then crosses the Middle Fork of the Yuba. Farther south, the road travels along sheer cliffs and is considered one of America's most exciting roads

Alleghany. Streets are on the side of a hill. Ground slopes away steeply behind these buildings on Alleghany's main street to Kanaka Creek below. The famous Sixteen to One Mine operates here. Fire destroyed most of town in 1933

One is the Henness Pass Road, the easier and quicker of the two. To reach it, you double back from Alleghany to Pliocene Ridge. Follow the road west to rejoin Highway 49 at Oregon Creek on the Middle Fork of the Yuba. Along this route you trace the path of emigrants and Concord coaches. The road is fairly narrow, but you can drive in high gear at about 30 miles per hour. Logging traffic is heavy, though, so watch for trucks.

The other exit is via the Foote Road which leads southwest from Alleghany through some of the most spectacular parts of the Northern Diggings. It is not a route for a timid driver. It is literally hewn out of the mountainside, and there are many places on this one-lane road where steep cliffs rise on one side and drop off hundreds of feet on the other. Second and low-gear stretches are numerous, and the turns are sharp. In some places the roadbed is supported by huge iron bars anchored in the cliff.

But for many, the drive is worth the hardship: The last stretch above Foote's Crossing has been called the most spectacular mile of mountain road in America.

Downieville

Fire and flood have done their best to destroy this mountain settlement, but Downieville is still one of the most entrancing gold towns left. The old stone, brick, and frame buildings, many of which were built in the 1860's or earlier, face on quiet, crooked streets which no longer hear the clatter and rumble of freighters or the din that hundreds, sometimes thousands, of miners could raise when they came to town for relaxation and a cup to slake their thirst.

Like many other camps along the forks of the Yuba, Downieville has contributed its share of true stories of rich strikes—like that of Tin Cup Diggings where three miners had little trouble filling a cup with dust each day, or of the 60-square-foot claim that gave up over $12,000 in eleven days, or of the 25-pound nugget of solid gold taken two miles above the camp.

There are several buildings which are almost as old as the stories. One is the present-day museum with walls of schist built in 1852, and another built in the same year is the Costa Store, which is a mortarless schist structure with walls four feet thick at the bottom.

In 1947 fire took the old courthouse and the St. Charles Hotel, built in 1853, whose overhanging roof and old locusts gave shade to loungers who could and would fill any interested traveler with the lore of the old days.

Many other buildings which were built in the 1860's cling to the mountainsides above the river. The lovely old residential section adds to the charm which makes Downieville the most picturesque county seat in California.

But it wasn't always quaint and quiet.

Downieville has the dubious distinction of being the only camp in the Gold Country to have hanged a woman. The story is clouded and even early newspaper accounts take violently opposing views on the lynching.

Some believe that Juanita, the fiery Mexican dance hall girl who plunged a knife into the breast of an annoying miner, acted in self-defense and was wrongfully lynched. Others claim that the stabbing was unprovoked and that she got what she deserved when they hauled her up on the hastily built gallows. No one will ever know whether she was actually with child as she claimed before they strung her up, or whether this would have made any difference to the mob. Right or wrong, the

Downieville. Here on picturesque Main Street you see typical Sunday "traffic," with the forested divide between the forks of the Yuba River rising in the background. The store at right, said to date from 1852, still buys gold from summer "snipers"

Downieville. Photo taken in 1861 by C. O. Phillips from his gallery on Main Street following a flood in spring of that year. Despite repeated floods and fires, Downieville still can claim to be one of the most picturesque of all the gold towns

Johnsville. View of the best preserved section of town. Although a latecomer as a gold mining camp—built in 1873—Johnsville is an interesting link in the Gold Country chain of old towns. There's enough snow here in the winter for organized skiing

Sierra City. One of the delights to children who travel through the Gold Country is the chance to explore abandoned buildings like this one built in 1871. Although landslide ruined the town in 1852, Sierra City has escaped devastation by fire

news electrified California, and Downieville has been on the defensive ever since.

Another story, often told, strikes a humorous vein. It seems that in 1850 a rascal was caught with a pair of stolen boots. The miners quickly gathered to hold court in the business place of the justice of the peace—a saloon. The culprit's guilt was established, but instead of a flogging or worse, he was ordered to buy the house drinks. After several rounds, the guilty one went unnoticed as he quietly left taking with him Exhibit A, the boots, and leaving behind the bill for the drinks.

Sierra City

The towering, jagged Sierra Buttes, which can be seen for scores of miles in all directions, overshadow the half-ghost town of Sierra City.

These dramatic granite peaks were tunneled through by Sierra City miners between 1850 and 1852 following the discovery of a quartz ledge, but in that winter, an avalanche of ice and snow crushed every shack and tent in the community. Even though it was several years before the town was rebuilt, the magnificent buttes continued to yield up their wealth.

There are several structures of an early vintage in Sierra City, and you are sure to see the Busch Building which was built in 1871—two stories of brick and a third of lumber.

Sierra Buttes. Magnificent crags overlook Upper Sardine Lake. They can be seen from Sierra City and for dozens of miles around. Miners drove tunnels into the Buttes as early as 1852 in the frantic search for gold-bearing rock

Near Sierraville. Summer range in the almost treeless reaches of the Sierra. Much interesting country surrounds the regions touched upon in this book, particularly the mid and high Sierra areas to the east of Highway 49

Over one of the doorways, you will see carved the initials E. C. V.—for E Clampus Vitus, the rollicking fraternity that captured the Gold Country.

It's not quite certain where the Clampers started—some say it was in Pennsylvania—but for California at least, it's sure that Sierra City was the birthplace.

Perhaps no fraternity in history gathered members in droves as E Clampus Vitus did in town after town. In many communities a man would have a hard time conducting business if he were not a member.

But hazing and hoaxing aside, the Clampers quietly went about helping the needy—widows, orphans, the sick and destitute. The charity was always anonymous, but the many letters of thanks that were printed in the newspapers of the day attest to the regard in which the pranksters were held.

E Clampus Vitus has been revived, and you will find plaques placed by modern Clampers to mark historical spots or to honor pioneers all through the Gold Country.

Johnsville

The best-preserved wooden town in the Northern Mines —or the Mother Lode for that matter—is Johnsvillle, about 12 miles by the crow flight or 40 miles via Highways 49 and 89 from Sierra City. But as a mining camp, it is a latecomer, relatively speaking, having been built in 1873 by a company of London investors who bought up claims in the vicinity.

There are many old buildings in various stages of collapse, and the spot is an excellent one for the photographers.

Plumas Eureka State Park

Encircling the historic old mining town of Johnsville, Plumas Eureka State Park is situated in one of the most scenic areas of Plumas County. Eureka Peak, Mt. Washington, and Mt. Elwell tower above the park's deep-cut, granite-walled canyons. There are a number of creeks and several small lakes. Jamison Creek emerges from the most prominent gorge. At an elevation of 6300 feet, Eureka Lake nestles in a glacial basin on the side of Eureka Peak. The park has improved camping areas.

An outstanding feature of the park is the gigantic old Stamp Mill used by the old Plumas Eureka Mining Company to grind out millions of dollars in gold. Ore came from the "drifts" reached by the several miles of tunnels that have been bored into the sides of Eureka Peak. Some of these tunnels were begun a century ago.

Restoration of this mill has been a major project of the Division of Beaches and Parks. Sections of the tunnels are being restored, as well as drifts and ore car tram lines, so that visitors can see vividly what the hard rock gold mining of the early days was like.

An old boarding house from those days has been transformed into a museum on mining, where you can see pioneer artifacts on display. You can see tools and hand-made gold mining equipment that was in common use during the last century.

WOODLEAF . . familiar sight

NEAR GIBSONVILLE . . old mine

FORBESTOWN . . lodge hall close-up

LA PORTE . braced against the snow

LA PORTE HIGHWAY . . cattle drive

FEATHER RIVER . . spectacular views

Howland Flat to Rich Bar
FEATHER RIVER AREA
OROVILLE · CHEROKEE · RICH BAR · BIDWELLS BAR
FEATHER FALLS · FORBESTOWN · WOODLEAF
STRAWBERRY VALLEY · LA PORTE
GIBSONVILLE · HOWLAND FLAT

Oroville

From 1849 through the 1870's, Oroville was a vigorous, boisterous mining town. Thereafter it was known to most travelers only as a quiet, tree-shaded town in the heart of thousands of acres of olive, citrus, and deciduous fruit orchards. But the whole area has now been brought to life again by "White Gold"—vast water projects on the Feather River, particularly the $490,000,000 Oroville Dam Project.

As in many other gold towns, placers were first worked by hand, then by hydraulic mining until it was outlawed. Since dredging operations began in 1898, the clawing buckets have taken more than $50,000,000. The ancient river bed on which Oroville is built is so rich in gold that a dredging company once offered to move the whole town just for the right to the ground on which it stood.

In the 1870's, Oroville's Chinese population was second only to that of San Francisco's Chinatown—and mining was the chief concern. But today, unless you stop and look around, you will see little more than a hint of Oroville's gold boom.

Perhaps the most interesting visit you could make in Oroville is to the Chinese temple—all that remains of the once-crowded Chinatown. The temple buildings, which are open to the public, were built in the 1850's. On display there are shrines, sedan chairs, tapestries, lamps, gongs, carvings, and other magnificent museum pieces.

Another valuable stop for those interested in Gold Rush history is the Pioneer and Relics Building. Here you can see many early-day tools and implements commonly used in the area at one time and, in addition, numbers of old photographs and documents.

North of Oroville is a rock structure known as the

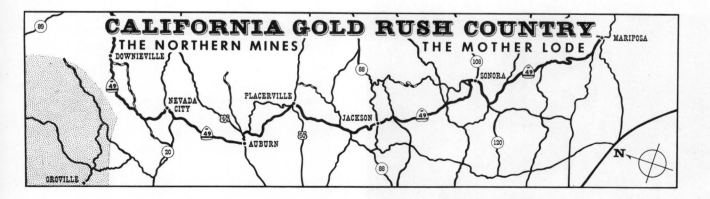

Oroville. This Chinese temple, known also as a joss house, was built in the 1850's during the Gold Rush. The thousands of Chinese who lived here through the 1870's have vanished, but this remnant has been restored and is used as a museum

Rich Bar. True to its name, Rich Bar made wealthy men out of some of the hardy ones who ventured up the Feather River Canyon in the early 1850's. Site would long ago have passed into obscurity if it hadn't been for the "Shirley Letters"

La Porte. Forest Service maintains an eight-stove campground near La Porte. The road is typical of better roads in the high country. Most of the many other campgrounds near the Gold Country are to the east of Highway 49

Chinese Wall—actually built by Italians rather than Chinese. It was constructed over a ten-year period after placer mining operations had depleted the richer and more accessible river deposits and was intended to divert the flow of the Feather River so that gravel in the river bed might be worked.

Although the project was abandoned before completion, some 10,000 cubic yards of materials went into its construction. The wall is about three-quarters of a mile in length and tapers from approximately 12 feet at the base to four feet at the top. In some places, it is 20 feet high.

To reach the Chinese Wall, turn off Highway 40 at the upper Thermalito bridge in Oroville and drive north toward Chico. When you come to the intersection at Cherokee Road (one mile northwest of Oroville), turn right on that road. The wall is about a mile farther.

Cherokee

About twelve miles beyond the Chinese Wall is the settlement of Cherokee. This area was the scene of extensive hydraulic mining operations and, in the year 1870 alone, produced about $5,000,000 in gold. A few diamonds were also discovered in this area at one time, but the resulting excitement was relatively short lived.

Bidwells Bar. First suspension bridge built west of Rockies (below) was removed at the start of Oroville Reservoir filling. New Bidwell Bar Bridge, now highest highway bridge in the world, is one half mile up river

All that's left of the frenzied mining days are some marks of the hydraulic mining: a great scar on Table Mountain, visible for miles; and rusting pipe lines and debris, some overgrown with shrubs and brush, scattered about the mountain.

North of Cherokee are the gold towns of Yankee Hill, Magalia (once known as Dogtown), Paradise, and Nimshew. Paradise, incidentally, was originally called

Pair o' Dice, but the name has mellowed along with the town.

Rich Bar

Rich Bar, which is over 50 miles from Oroville up the scenic Feather River Highway, has a double claim for its place in history.

First is the fact that Rich Bar was the scene of the greatest gold strike in the Feather River Canyon. Before it was sluiced out, somewhere between $14 and $23 million was taken from the gravels there. Old histories tell of a miner named Greenwood who first panned there in July of 1850 and from his first two pans took $2,900.

Although nothing but the foundations of one old building remains today, at its height Rich Bar boasted a population of over 2,500. The camp was appropriately named, for the gravel was so rich that claims were limited to *ten feet square.*

Rich Bar's second claim, and in the long run perhaps the more important bid for lasting fame, is based on the famed *Shirley Letters*—the vivid chronicle of early gold camp life written by Mrs. Louise Amelia Clapp in the years 1851 and 1852 when the lived in the rough and desolate outpost with her husband, a physician.

These letters, which were first published in 1854 in a San Francisco monthly magazine, were written to her sister at their old home in Amhurst, Massachusetts, and were signed "Dame Shirley." Although they were not originally written for publication, they are considered the best eye-witness account of early Gold Rush camp life in existence.

Bidwells Bar

In July of 1848, John Bidwell, California pioneer who later founded the city of Chico on his great Sacramento Valley ranch, made one of the major discoveries of the Gold Rush when he uncovered a deposit of raw gold below the junction of the Middle and South Forks of

Strawberry Valley. Old barn is one of several that mark the old stage stop on the Marysville-La Porte turnpike. Busy stores and saloons lined the road in the days when six-in-hand Concord stagecoaches thundered along this route

the Feather River. His find opened up all the rich Feather River country for exploitation.

Bidwells Bar was also the site of the first suspension bridge west of the Rockies. The bridge was removed at the start of the Oroville Dam project, and the old bridge site is now inundated by the reservoir.

Oroville. North of Oroville is the rock structure known as Chinese Wall. It cost $12,000,000 to build and took over ten years to finish. Purpose of the wall was to divert the Feather River so that its bed might be worked for gold

Feather Falls. This plumelike cascade of the Fall River, plunges 640 feet in a single leap. Located near the junction with the Middle Fork of the Feather River, it lends its name to the newly-developing scenic area

There is a story about the construction of the bridge that should be preserved as a tribute to pioneer ingenuity.

The parts of the bridge were fabricated in New York, shipped around the Horn, and carted from San Francisco by ox-drawn wagon. All that remained was to fit the parts together. Construction went smoothly until the engineer, a Mr. Evans, found that there was nothing with which to anchor the cables to the rock piers. But he wasn't stopped for long. At that time, tea was shipped from China to California in bales wrapped in huge sheets of lead foil, and Evans hired small boys to collect this foil, paying them 25c a pound for it. When enough had been collected, it was melted and used to imbed the ends of cables into the piers.

Beyond Bidwells Bar, the road leads through Berry Creek and Brush Creek along the old Oroville-Quincy stage route. It passes Bucks Lake and the 1850 mining camp of Spanish Ranch eight miles west of Quincy.

Feather Falls

Deep in the Feather River logging country about 23 miles east of Oroville, is the lumber town of Feather Falls. The magnificent falls for which the town was named are about four and a half miles from the village.

For the most direct approach to the falls, leave Highway 70 (formerly U.S. Highway 40 Alternate) at Oroville, on Oro Dam Boulevard, and take the Olive Highway east for 10 miles to Lake Wyandotte and the junction with Lumpkin Road. Drive 13 miles northeast, look for a sign on the left indicating the side road to Feather Falls; follow this road for 2 miles to its end at Bryant Ravine. It's a 3-mile hike from there to the falls.

La Porte

If you travel east from Oroville through Forbestown, you will intersect the road that follows the Marysville-La Porte stage route near Challenge. East lies the remote Sierra country between the Yuba and Feather rivers.

The Challenge-La Porte area is, because of its soil, one of the best pine-growing areas in California. Ask at the Challenge Ranger Station about side trips into perfect stands of sugar pine.

Heading east on the road, you pass through old stage stops—Woodleaf, Clipper Mills, Strawberry Valley—and climb higher into the granite hills to La Porte and beyond to the wind-swept redoubt of Gibsonville.

La Porte, which was a well-populated hydraulic mining center before the Anti-Debris Act was passed, may be remembered longer as the place where little Lotta Crabtree scored her first success dancing and singing for miners on a rough board stage.

If instead of starting your trip to La Porte at Challenge, you begin about 25 miles farther south on the old stage route at Browns Valley, you can get a clearer running view of California trees from the Central Valley to the high Sierra than most roads can give.

First are the valley oaks, cottonwoods, sycamores, alders. Next come the interior live oaks and digger pines of the foothills. Then you'll find the tan oak, madrone, chinquapin, and the mixed forest of incense cedar, Douglas fir, ponderosa pine, sugar pine, and white fir. Finally, at the higher elevation you'll find red fir and some foxtail pine mixed with the ponderosa and sugar pines.

Gibsonville. Perched on a wind-swept ridge overlooking Slate Creek, a few bleached houses mark the site of Gibsonville. Here, as at La Porte, the houses are braced with poles against the heavy winter snow load

Howland Flat. Town (population summer 10, winter 1) can be reached by a 10-mile, rocky but safe road which drops 1,100 feet into Slate Canyon and then climbs 2,000 feet in six miles to reach 6,000 feet at Howland Flat. Site of Poker Flat three miles away

Index

Single page numbers refer to principal references. Numbers in parentheses refer to pages on which additional photographs will be found.

Photo Credits

Front cover (Nevada City Firehouse) by Glenn Christiansen. Frontispiece by Clyde Childress. Back cover (Kennedy Mine tailing wheels, Jackson Gate) and title page (Fallon House Theater, Columbia) by Martin Litton. Photographs on the foldout map by Martin Litton, Clyde Childress, Ray Atkeson, and George Ballis.

Photographs in this book by the following: **Marilyn Bronson:** pages 26 (top left), 28 (bottom), 49 (bottom), 52 (top right). **William Bronson:** pages 20 (bottom left), 27, 28 (top right), 39 (top right, bottom left), 42 (bottom left), 44 (top left, center), 46 (top right), 48 (center), 49 (top), 53, 54 (bottom), 56 (top), 57 (top right), 60 (bottom right), 62 (top), 63 (bottom), 64, 65 (top), 67 (top), 85 (top right), 87. Courtesy of **California Historical Society, San Francisco:** pages 17 (top left), 39 (top left), 74 (bottom), 93 (bottom). **Clyde Childress:** pages 19 (bottom), 24 (bottom), 40 (top), 44 (top and bottom right), 45 (top and bottom right), 46 (top left, center right), 54 (top), 55 (top right), 56 (center), 57 (bottom), 58 (right), 59 (bottom left), 60 (center and bottom left), 62 (bottom), 66 (bottom), 68 (bottom right), 70 (bottom left), 72 (top and bottom left), 84, 85 (top left), 90 (center left, bottom), 94 (bottom right). **Patricia Cullen:** page 72 (top right). **Dan Erickson:** page 94 (bottom right). **Victor Hake:** page 98 (top left). **Walter Houk:** pages 22, 23 (top), 25 (top right). **Martin Litton:** pages 12, 14, 15, 16, 17 (top right, bottom), 18, 19 (top), 20 (top left, center, bottom right), 23 (bottom), 24 (top), 25 (top left, bottom), 26 (top right, bottom), 29, 30, 31, 32, 39 (bottom right), 40 (bottom), 41, 42 (top, bottom right), 43, 44 (bottom left), 45 (top left), 46 (center left, bottom), 48 (top), 50 (top and bottom left), 51, 52 (top and bottom left), 55 (bottom), 56 (bottom), 58 (left), 59 (top), 60 (top, center right), 63 (top), 66 (top), 67 (bottom), 68 (top, bottom left), 69, 70 (top, center, bottom right), 73 (bottom), 74 (top), 75, 76, 77, 78 (top, bottom right), 81, 82 (bottom), 83, 85 (bottom), 86 (top, center right, bottom), 88, 90 (center right), 92 (top), 93 (top), 94 (top and bottom left), 95, 96 (top left, center, bottom right), 98 (top right), 100. **Theodore Osmundson:** pages 65 (bottom), 92 (center, bottom), 98 (bottom). **Phil Palmer:** pages 73 (top), 78 (bottom left). **Louise Pfeiffer:** page 50 (top right). **George Pfeiffer III:** page 57 (top left). **John Robinson:** pages 78 (center right), 81, 82 (center), 86 (center left), 89, 96 (top left, bottom right), 98 (center), 99, 101. **Sidney Smith:** page 59 (bottom right).